IID661316

O^{The}rganized
ADMIN

Julie Perrine
CAP®-OM, MBTI® Certified,
Certified Productivity Pro® Consultant

Founder of All Things Admin
A Julie Perrine International, LLC Company

AllThingsAdmin.com
TheOrganizedAdmin.com

The Organized ADMIN

Leverage Your Unique Organizing Style to Create Systems, Reduce Overwhelm, and Increase Productivity

Julie Perrine
CAP®-OM, MBTI® Certified,
Certified Productivity Pro® Consultant

Founder of All Things Admin
A Julie Perrine International, LLC Company

AllThingsAdmin.com
TheOrganizedAdmin.com

Dedication

To Evelyn Nuehring –
One of the most positive, upbeat, and courageous women
I've ever known.

Your living example of perseverance and a positive attitude
in the face of adversity have encouraged me to have faith,
push forward, and be grateful for the people and lessons that
come from this journey of life.

Table of Contents

Foreword

The phone call was routine. I asked my usual assessment questions:

"What is the primary goal?"

"I need to set up my office space so it is used efficiently."

"What is the primary change that needs to take place?"

"I need to clear out all the excess papers and set up systems."

"What are you most concerned about?"

"I need to calm down my workspace. When I try to look for things, I have to move other things."

And that was the beginning of my relationship with Julie Perrine.

Julie is always looking for the most effective and efficient means of doing things. If there is a way to shorten the learning curve, she wants to find it. That is why Julie and I began working together. And that is why I have worked with her in her first office, second office, home office, and in other areas of her personal and professional life. Always open to my coaching, she was a quick learner and willing to make changes to achieve her organizing goals.

Fast-forward 10 years, and Julie has written a book inspired by many of the organization principles I have taught her. And I am so proud of my dedicated and hard-working student.

I often tell my clients the best way to learn something new is to do it. This concept is called praxis. The beautiful thing about this book is that, through her writing, Julie guides you in a simple and straightforward way to use praxis to accomplish your organizing goals.

Each chapter is dedicated to an area of your work life that requires organization, whether it is the physical appearance of your workspace, your email, or the complicated travel schedule of your executive. Julie clearly describes the possible issues you may face and systematically provides clear and meaningful solutions to solve these challenges. Her plan of action at the end of each chapter reduces overwhelm by providing a step-by-step approach to improving organization in that particular area.

> *"Being organized is not an end in itself – it is*
> *a vehicle to take you*
> *from where you are to where you want to be."*
> ~ STEPHANIE WINSTON, AUTHOR OF
> *THE ORGANIZED EXECUTIVE*

It is important to understand that improving your organization skills is mostly about behavior modification. You have to change your habits to change your environment. So I encourage you to recognize your natural strengths and use them in the organizing processes highlighted in this book.

I often ask my clients, "What is causing you the most discomfort right now?" The answer to that question helps me to determine our starting point. Ask yourself that question, then pick the chapter of this book that corresponds with your concern.

What impresses me most about this book is that Julie wrote it from her head and her heart. I have had the honor of coaching her throughout the writing process, and it is very clear that her drive to put these words on paper is to help as many people as she possibly can. I promise that if you take even one recommendation from this book, you will become a better administrative assistant.

Congratulations on taking the first step to a more organized life!

Maggie Jackson, CPO®
President and Owner
The Organized Life
Certified Professional Organizer®
NAPO Golden Circle Member®
ICD Level II Chronic Disorganization Specialist
ICD Level II Attention Deficit Disorder Specialist

Getting Started

Welcome to *The Organized Admin*!

When I launched All Things Admin in 2009, I began asking assistants, "What are your top two challenges?" Over and over again, the answer has been, "Getting organized!" Admins want help organizing time, spaces, files, emails, meetings, events, travel, projects, their careers, and more!

In this book, I am going to address the key areas where organizing challenges arise for admins and explain:

- What it means to "be organized."

- Why being organized is vital to your career success.

- How to become more organized in your career.

- Tools and systems that may help you stay organized.

- Tips and resources you can apply to your environment and work style.

Review the Roadmap and Chart Your Course

To get started using this book, scan through the table of contents to gain an overview of the topics covered in becoming The Organized Admin. As you scan it, flag or highlight the chapters you want to focus on first. Most chapters contain an action plan at the end to give you a roadmap for getting started and taking immediate action.

Once you have a good overview of the material, use this book as a guide to chart your course to organization. You may want to break the process down into weekly or monthly goals. Track your progress to help you stay the course.

The chapters of this book and areas of organization were inspired by survey responses and reader feedback from the past several years. However, if you have an organizing challenge in an area the book doesn't cover, please let me know! Send me a message through the Contact page at **TheOrganizedAdmin.com**, and tell me what you need help with. I love hearing from you, and I'd love to help you find a solution!

Your Implementation Plan

For your convenience, all of the action plans in this book (plus a binder cover) are available in an electronic download at **TheOrganizedAdmin.com**. I did this so you can easily download the action plans, put them in a three-ring binder (The Organized Admin binder!), and use them to track your personal progress and transformation as you implement what you learn.

I also recommend you start a journal or insert blank sheets of lined paper in your binder so you can record things as you work through each chapter. You'll need something to take notes on and capture thoughts in as you're inspired by the various examples and ideas in this book. Having your action plans and writing paper in the same binder will keep you organized.

Additionally, I encourage you to take before-and-after pictures of your workspace or screenshots of your digital file folders to include in your binder so you can see the progress you make along the way. You may not want to remember how awful it looked when you first began, but it's a key motivator when you look at it later and see how far you've come. I even encourage taking pictures at various stages of the process to track your journey visually. It's a very powerful way to view your progress from start to finish.

Resources, Files, and What I Use

Throughout this book, you'll find these three icons indicating additional resources, files, or ideas for that chapter. Since organizing products and technologies often change, I didn't want to list the specific product brands or names in print. Instead, I've posted links and pictures on our website, **TheOrganizedAdmin.com**, so you can always find the latest tools I use and recommend.

 The file folder icon indicates a **File Download.**

 The mouse icon indicates a **Resource Alert.**

 The push pin icon indicates **What I Use.**

My Writing Style

I tend to write in a conversational style. While I do believe in good grammar, correct punctuation, and complete sentences, there may be places where I stray a bit for emphasis. But fear not – my editing team usually keeps me in line. I share this because I know how particular admins, myself included, can be. It is, after all, part of what we do for a living – proofing other people's documents. That said, if you find an error that I should correct in future editions, please visit the Contact page at **TheOrganizedAdmin.com** and let me know.

Throughout the book, the terms "admin," "assistant," and "administrative professional" are used to represent the hundreds of titles that comprise the administrative profession. No matter what your specific title may be, I've written this book for you. I also use the terms "manager," "executive," "boss," "supervisor," and "team" when referring to those you work with or report to – no matter what their titles may be.

Let's Get Organized

A lot of what I'm going to share and recommend may require making changes to how you currently work. It will require establishing new habits and eliminating old ones that are not supporting you. There are no shortcuts. You have to do the work to experience the results of change and transformation that you are looking for in your life and career.

At times, my approach is direct and to the point. But if you have heard me speak, participated in my training programs, or follow my writing online, you know I always tackle issues with a positive, proactive attitude. This book is no exception.

If you're ready to finally get organized, let's get started!

Part 1: Organization Basics

Before we can dive into specific ways to help you organize things, we need to cover a few basics that will set you up for long-term organizing success!

- What Does "Organized" Mean?

- The Cost of Disorganization

- Discover Your Unique Organizing Style

- Principles of Organization

- Create Systems for Organization

Chapter 1

What Does "Organized" Mean?

"Organization is neither entirely genetic nor environmental; it's learned. This is reassuring because no one is perfectly organized."
~ LAURA STACK, THE PRODUCTIVITY PRO®,
BEST-SELLING AUTHOR, AND SPEAKER

Being organized means something different to everyone. Yet as administrative professionals, getting and staying organized are essential to being effective and efficient in our professional roles…and maintaining our sanity.

When people walk up to our desks, they expect us to know the answers, find the information they need, or connect them to the right people or resources. The ability to put our hands on that information and deliver it as quickly as possible builds credibility, trust, and confidence in those we support. Conversely, when we can't find what we need, miss important details, or don't have a good system in place, we look incompetent and create a level of distrust that can be difficult to overcome.

The problem with getting organized is that people often think of it as a destination or a project, when it's actually an ongoing practice. It's not a place you arrive at and then quit. It's a habit you develop. It's a skill you learn. You have to continually exercise discipline and practice organizing your time, work, and things.

We all have an area or two where we need to improve. There may be people who appear to have it all together in one area, but I guarantee there are other places in their lives that are disorganized. I'm a good example of this. I've had several people tell me I'm the most organized person they know. And I do a pretty good job in most areas, but I have organizing challenges just like everyone else. Each time I advanced to a new level of responsibility or executive support, I had to adjust my organization strategies for the new situation. While I've always kept my work office organized, I struggled with my home office when I started my business. Advances in technology and software force me to reevaluate my organization systems more frequently.

Thankfully, I met Maggie Jackson, a Certified Professional Organizer. With Maggie's assistance, I came to understand the immense value of a professional organizer – even for the most organized admins. She helped me identify my organizing problem spots, create a plan for resolving them, and develop new habits that made it easier to maintain an organized space in my new environment moving forward.

Maggie also taught me that getting organized means letting go of one major myth: organized doesn't mean neat. And she's right. If your organizing style is to put everything away and my style is to keep everything out, our desks are going to look very different. Neither style is wrong. But one style will look neater, even though both are organized and effective for our respective work styles. As you'll learn in this book, being organized doesn't necessarily mean your desk is perfectly arranged – it means you can find what you need when you need it.

So, as you start thinking about organization, try to let go of the perfectionist mindset. Realize it's OK to ask for help. Understand that the principles of organization are the same no matter where you go, but you might need to adjust how you apply them. And most importantly, accept that getting organized is an ongoing and evolutionary process.

Organization Defined

I define organization as the systems we use to find, do, or complete things. Whether you're looking for a file at the office or gloves in your coat closet, the system you use to help you store and locate things is key.

As I've worked with professional organizers throughout my career, it always comes down to one question: "Where does this item live?" If it doesn't have a permanent home or system for quick retrieval, then you need to create one. That's one secret to eliminating clutter, getting organized, and maintaining a healthy level of organization that will support you moving forward.

This is why I love creating office procedures and developing forms, templates, and checklists to help me stay on top of each project, task, or assignment. This is also why I keep a few simple tools at the ready so I can quickly sort, contain, and label items and create a home for them. (We'll talk more about those things later in this book.)

When you approach organization with the understanding that it's a skill you can learn and a habit you can develop regardless of your tendencies, and you create effective systems to support an organized environment moving forward, it creates a new perspective that will help you get and stay organized.

If you're ready, let's get started!

PLAN OF ACTION:

☐ Make a list of the organizing problem spots you have today.

☐ Jot down some notes about why they are a challenge, and what keeps you from getting or maintaining organization in your problem spots.

☐ Note your answers to the above questions in your journal or organization binder.

☐ Share your challenges with us at **TheOrganizedAdmin.com**.

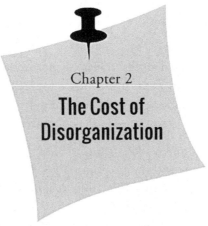

Chapter 2

The Cost of Disorganization

"Clutter is not just the stuff on your floor – it's anything that stands between you and the life you want to be living."
~ Peter Walsh, professional organizer,
author, and media personality

As an administrative professional, you know being organized is crucial to your effectiveness. But have you ever thought about why? Has disorganization ever caused you to waste time? Or money? Have you ever thought about the cost of disorganization to your company? What many people don't take into account is the adverse effect that disorganization can have not only on a job and career, but an entire office.

Disorganization comes at measurable costs of time, money, and overall resources. Consider these startling statistics:

- In a survey conducted by Brother International Corporation, the average worker spends 38 hours per year looking for out-of-place things. That's almost a full workweek![1]

- The estimated annual dollars spent searching for lost files or misplaced items in the office tops $89 billion among full-time office professionals. This doesn't even include searching for lost files on the computer.[2]

- One-in-three workers say they "somewhat" or "very" often must spend time reprinting previously created documents because they have been misplaced.[3]

When you convert the cost of lost time and wasted resources into dollars and cents, it's staggering!

Disorganization Spells Disaster

Missing a deadline here or there or being slightly disorganized may not sound like that big of a deal to some. But one assistant's disorganization almost cost PepsiCo $1.26 billion.[4] Can you imagine?

In June 2009, a legal summons and complaint was served on one of the company's registered agents and then forwarded to an attorney at PepsiCo's New York headquarters. The attorney's administrative assistant received the information, but she did not handle the documents according to the established system and no immediate action was taken. Because PepsiCo did not respond to the summons and complaint in a timely manner, the opposing side filed for a default judgment against PepsiCo in the amount of $1.26 billion. PepsiCo eventually was able to get the default judgment vacated. But think about the time and expense that was then spent on fixing the issue created by this assistant's disorganization. This is an incredible example of the cost that disorganization of one person in your office can have on the entire company.

You've heard the saying "time is money." The more disorganized you are, the more time you waste, and the more money you and your company lose. You can't keep your executive and team on track and organized if you're not organized yourself. Disorganization can cause you to miss deadlines, overlook tasks, and forget about important details. "One of the biggest ways companies lose money is poor use of time," says Jennifer Snyder, owner of Neat as a Pin Organizing Experts. "Disorganized processes and employees can be an insidious drain on the bottom line."[5] In other words, wasted time due to disorganization means wasted money, which in excess can damage your employer's long-term profitability and success.

A 2011 Express Employment Professionals survey of more than 18,000 business leaders revealed that 57% of respondents said they lose six work hours per week due to disorganization.[6] The survey also concluded that disorganized employees who make $50,000 annually could cost their companies an estimated $11,000 per year in lost time due to their disorganization.[7] Don't let this happen to you!

The Clutter Factor

Clutter, whether it's tactile or electronic, has a profound and palpable effect on an office. According to the Brother survey, 87% of workers surveyed said cluttered spaces made them feel less productive, and 86% thought a disorganized workspace was unprofessional.[8]

Clutter can also damage your professional reputation and credibility. In a 2011 OfficeMax Workspace Organization Survey, 38% of respondents said clutter negatively affected their professional image, and 77% said their productivity was impacted.[9] A CareerBuilder survey also found that even if workers were actually working on multiple projects with positive results, workplace clutter was causing employers to have a negative view of them. Nearly 38% of employers said piles of paper covering a desk negatively impacted their perception of that person.[10] That means the chaos on your desk is not only impacting your productivity, but quite possibly your opportunities for advancement, too!

Look around your desk and workspace right now. How cluttered is your area? Consciously think about how you feel every time you see all of those sticky notes or knick-knacks. It's a drain mentally and emotionally – whether you realize it or not. Researchers at the Princeton University Neuroscience Institute found that when your environment is cluttered, the chaos restricts your ability to focus. Clutter also distracts you and limits your brain's ability to process information.[11]

I challenge you to take five minutes right now and clear all of the clutter from your workspace. Tape those sticky notes to a sheet of three-hole punched paper and put them in your procedures binder. (Create one if you don't have one.) Put all of the little mementos you've collected on your desk into a box and place it under your desk. Then sit back down at your desk and observe how it looks and makes you feel. It's a much different feeling, isn't it? That's the impact of clutter.

When you combine how your clutter makes you feel with how others perceive you because of it, it's a motivating force to pursue a clutter-free space.

Organization and Stress

The cost of disorganization goes beyond measurable losses, such as time and money, and damage to your reputation. It can also add significant stress, which can further damage your professional image. If you're a disorganized, frazzled mess, it can have a big effect on how you're perceived professionally around the office – both by your peers and executives. And this negativity can lead to even higher stress levels.

Getting organized can literally help you breathe easier during your workday, lower your stress, and contribute to better health. Disorganization can cost you a lot of time and money, and put your job, career, and well-being at risk. You have everything to gain by improving your organization skills, and a lot to lose if you don't.

PLAN OF ACTION:

☐ Identify the disorganized areas that are wasting time, costing money, and/or creating stress.

☐ Share your disorganization problem spots with us at **TheOrganizedAdmin.com.**

☐ Look around your desk and workspace, and identify the different types of clutter (sticky notes, coffee cups, office supplies, knick knacks, photos).

☐ Take a picture of your desk and workspace right now – before you clear any of the clutter.

☐ Take 10 minutes and clear all of the clutter from your workspace.

  ☐ Tape sticky notes to a sheet of three-hole-punched paper and put them in your procedures binder. (Create a procedures binder if you don't have one.)

  ☐ Put the office supplies away or create new homes for them.

  ☐ Put all of the knick-knacks and photos from your desk into a box and place it under your desk.

  ☐ Clear all bottles, mugs, and food

☐ Sit down at your desk and observe how it looks and how it makes you feel. Write a few notes about the thoughts and emotions this inspired for you. What do you think are the main reasons that clutter accumulates in your workspace? (Hint: Your answer will contain clues for how you can overcome clutter once and for all.)

☐ Take a picture of your desk and workspace after you clear the clutter. Compare the two pictures you've taken. How do you feel when you look at the before picture compared to the after picture?

☐ If you're willing, share your before-and-after pictures with us at **TheOrganizedAdmin.com**.

Chapter 3

Discover Your Unique Organizing Style

"The secret of being organized under any circumstances, and in any situation, is taking charge of your organizational styles rather than letting them take charge of you."
~ SUNNY SCHLENGER AND ROBERTA ROESCH,
AUTHORS OF *HOW TO BE ORGANIZED IN SPITE OF YOURSELF*

Have you ever wondered why some of your co-workers' desks are immaculate and others look like a tornado blew across them? If you're thinking these wind-swept desks are due to their owners' messiness, consider this: What if all that perceived chaos helps them be more organized?

Being organized doesn't always mean having everything put away or in neat piles. For some people (myself included), the best way to stay organized is by having everything out in front of them where it can be easily seen. This doesn't make them less organized – it just means their organization style preferences are different.

Just like you have a unique personality type, you also have an organizing style and a time management style that are all your own. And the two are actually tied together. Organizing your space and your time means more than just straightening up and becoming more productive – it can result in the overall improvement of your quality of living. Understanding how to make the best use of your natural tendencies and implementing the strategies, systems, and products that enhance your style will enable you to make choices that move you into a powerful state of flow.[12]

Strengths, Personality Types, and Style Preferences

Your personality type and your strengths have a big effect on how you manage time and how you get and stay organized. So it's extremely helpful if you identify and understand your style preferences before you create your plan for getting and staying organized.

To figure out your time management and organization style preferences, I highly recommend using the Time & Space Style Inventory (TSSI™), which was developed by Cena Block, Founder of Sane Spaces, LLC (sanespaces.com).

The TSSI is one of the most comprehensive and effective assessment tools available to help people understand their natural behaviors regarding their use of time and how they organize space. The online assessment tool was developed in close collaboration with Sunny Schlenger, the co-author of the original book, *How to Be Organized In Spite of Yourself* (out of print) and author of *Flow Formula: A Guidebook to Wholeness and Harmony*. The tool not only provides a style report that will help you better understand your style strengths, but it also provides access to an online database with videos, tools, and suggestions on how technology and other solutions can help (or hinder) you depending on your specific preference mix – what Block calls your Unique Flow Formula.

Your Style Preference™ is determined by your natural behaviors related to time and space management. Just as your personality type is distinctive, your TSSI style scores will also be unique to you. A style preference is typically characterized by consistent behaviors demonstrated over time. There is no "right" or "wrong" style preference; no "good" one or "bad" one. The inventory simply measures degrees of preference. Most people demonstrate natural tendencies that represent unique combinations of different style preferences. The scores themselves matter less than the information they reveal and the insights you will gain by looking deeper at your typical behaviors, habits, and patterns that you've developed over time.

There are six primary Space Style Preferences and six primary Time Style Preferences.

Time Style Preferences

Your Time Style Preferences describe how you manage your days, hours, and minutes. They are based on how you handle your priorities, attend to details, and deal with action items.

The Time Style Preferences include:

- **Hopper:** These people enjoy change of pace and the ability to switch from one task to another. For Hoppers, switch-tasking can be very exhilarating as long as they don't have too many open tasks at one time. They tend to be easily distracted, so they run the risk of getting pulled off-track and not finishing what they start. Although they typically claim their excellence at multitasking, too many open tasks at one time can be really unproductive because it tends to delay completing any one task. So it's important to eliminate distractions and schedule chunks of time to finish tasks. A timer can be a Hopper's best friend.

- **Hyper Focus:** Hyper Focus people tend to become absorbed in the details and often have trouble stopping one activity and transitioning to another. They ignore reminders and frequently lose track of time. More than any other Time Style Preferences, those who score strong and/or dominant in this style have the best results when they operate on a schedule and create strategies to help them transition from task to task. Backward planning and scheduling can also be helpful.

- **Big Picture:** Big Picture individuals think big yet have a tendency to leave out details. They can find the small stuff to be less relevant than big strategies and master plans. This lofty mindset can cause essential small tasks to be overlooked or ignored. A Big Picture personality works better when partnered with people who can sweat the details and tactics for them. A basic scheduling approach with ongoing routine tasks helps these folks stay on top of maintenance tasks, and writing things down is an essential strategy to support their Time Style Preference.

- **Perfectionist Plus:** Perfectionist Plus personalities thrive on details and work hard to get things right. They tend to have very high personal standards, and believe they can do everything themselves (and do it very well). These types can use their time more efficiently when they learn to distinguish between high- and low-priority activities.

Prioritizing activities based on a given task's payoff will help them manage their need to get it right, with their drive to get it done. A crucial time management strategy for a Perfectionist Plus personality is to say "no" and delegate to trusted support people when possible.

- **Impulsive:** Impulsives like the rush of adrenaline and tend to leap before they look. Their desire for spontaneity, and tendency toward reactivity, can make it challenging for them to follow a preset plan, which can lead to missed deadlines and letting people down. This personality tends to get bored easily with mundane tasks and therefore may resist routines. For Impulsives to get a grasp on the bigger picture, they need to learn to make better decisions. Posting mantras, reminders, and goals can help remind them to stay focused.

- **Cliff Hanger:** Cliff Hangers believe that they work most effectively when under the pressure of a deadline. They like having an adrenaline rush to help them focus, but this often doesn't leave enough time to check work thoroughly or to handle things that might go wrong. Waiting to start until the last moment often causes added stress, tension, and even missed deadlines. Cliff Hangers need to monitor their time and estimate how long it will take to finish a project or task. They can benefit from identifying their highest-priority tasks and scheduling early start dates, using milestones for partial completion instead of completion dates.

When I went through the book and inventory, I learned that my dominant Time Style Preferences were Hopper and

Perfectionist Plus. Here's what this means for me, and probably some of you reading.

A Hopper naturally enjoys having many projects and tasks at a time because it helps them maintain their energy and motivation. That's me. The downside is I tend to get distracted (especially when I'm bored). Or worse yet, I get discouraged because I have so many open items going at once. So the key for me is setting myself up to hop well. As a Hopper, I need to pay attention to my energy levels so I can take breaks to maintain my focus and reduce the chance for distractions. This helps me finish things more successfully. A timer is definitely helpful in getting me to focus for set blocks of time.

As a Perfectionist Plus, it's important for me to create a to-do list and prioritize based on importance, enjoyability, and profitability. This way, I'm putting my best effort and perfectionist tendencies into the most important and most profitable items first. Then what's left over can be handled in a not-so-perfectionist style if I have to just plow through it to get things done and meet deadlines.

Space Style Preferences

Your Space Style Preferences reflect the ways you manage your surroundings. They are based on how you arrange your space, assign value to items, and tolerate disorder.

The TSSI identifies six Space Style Preferences, including:

- **Everything Out:** Everything Outs use visual cues as reminders and leave things out so they can find them easily. They fear that putting things away may cause them to forget to take action. But too many unattended items left out can quickly lead to a cluttered space, and it can become difficult for these people to find what they're looking for. Everything Outs do well to survey their desks often and make sure the visible items are only those they use and/or are pleasing to look at. They also do well with clear acrylic storage containers that help them "see what they have" in place of the typical opaque tubs or closed storage containers.

- **Nothing Out:** Nothing Outs equate a clear surface with being organized. They avoid what feels like clutter in visible spaces and prefer organization products that hide things from view. Because they dislike mess, they often stash items away in haste in drawers and closets. This behavior can be troublesome if inside spaces are unorganized and lack reliable systems for retrieval. Because of this tendency, it's necessary for them to devise and maintain organization and retrieval systems in their storage and hidden spaces. This style may find electronic planning and scheduling tools and apps especially appealing.

- **Saver:** Savers feel that virtually everything might come in handy someday. But saving becomes a problem when the volume of things saved overwhelms their space. They don't necessarily accept that the actual value of things tends to change over time, which can lead Savers to believe their collections are more valuable than they are. Savers will benefit from using a ranking system to determine what has the highest value to them. They also may need support to assist them in passing on items of lesser value. Savers do well by organizing in limited chunks of time or defined spaces so the decision-making process is not overwhelming.

- **Minimalist:** Minimalists dislike clutter and avoid it by letting go of items frequently, sometimes at the cost of sentimental value. They typically pass up "free" items and prefer to live in the moment. Minimalists should evaluate the importance of their belongings so meaningful personal items and items of value are not let go in haste. It's especially important for Minimalists to avoid disposing of others' belongings without permission just to lessen their tension!

- **Straightener:** Straighteners like to line things up and create neat piles, but straightened doesn't always mean organized. Straighteners tend to be so preoccupied with neatness that they sometimes don't recognize when their straightened arrangements may not make organizational sense. Because of their propensity for neatness, Straighteners need to distinguish between simple tidying and actual organizing. Their storage and retrieval systems should be easy to use and manage, and keep things neat as well as organized.

- **No Rules:** No Rules types may look more disorganized than they actually are due to a lack of systems and routine. Although they may know what they have and be able to find things, No Rules types typically have few, if any, systems to help them stay organized. No Rules people need to understand that changes can be gradually achieved with simple planning and the right products. They may need support to devise personal storage and retrieval systems that are convenient and easy to manage.

When I took the TSSI, I learned that my Space Style Flow Formula is a combination of Everything Out and Saver, which

I suspected. As an Everything Out person, I need a system for processing paper: incoming, outgoing, trash, to file, to read, to do, pending, etc. I need clear or translucent accessories and poly folders to help me keep things in focus, and not out of sight and therefore out of mind. As a Saver, it's very important that I create permanent homes for things so I can find them again later, and balance my kept items with the amount of available space I have. Color-coding is a great organization system that helps me accomplish that!

No matter what your Style Preferences may be, it's not something you should hide behind or use as an excuse. Assessment tools, like the Myers-Briggs Type Indicator®, DiSC®, Clifton StrengthsFinder®, TSSI, and others are designed to give us insights into our preferences. These insights help us become more self-aware so we can apply that knowledge to our work and our relationships.

Part of this new level of self-awareness is understanding how others may perceive our styles. With a Style Preference dominance of Everything Out, I have to realize that my desk may look messy or cluttered to those passing by. So I try to put extra effort into making sure what I do have visible on my desk is in neat piles or file sorters as much as possible. At the end of the day, I clear all of the stacks from my desk. That not only forces me to plan and prioritize for the next day, but it helps me maintain a more organized work space.

If you choose to take the TSSI – and I strongly encourage you to – your Score Report will help you get a handle on how you're naturally "wired up," and the suggested resources will help you design better systems to keep yourself organized based on the unique traits of your organization style. You may suggest that your executive take the assessment too! This information will also help you identify your executive's styles and preferences, which means you can support them more effectively. What works for you may not work for them, but you can adapt your approach and help them create order and organization out of their chaos.

Understanding your own organization style, as well as your executive's, won't just make you more organized – it will help you become a better administrative professional!

PLAN OF ACTION:

☐ Review the six Time Style Preferences. Which Time Style Preference(s) do you think are your most dominant?

☐ Review the six Space Style Preferences. Which Space Style Preference(s) do you think are your most dominant?

☐ Based on what you've read, what do you think your executive's most dominant Time Style and Space Style Preferences are?

☐ How are you and your executive the same? How are you different?

☐ If you'd like to verify your reported organization type by taking the TSSI, you can find the assessment link at **TheOrganizedAdmin.com.**

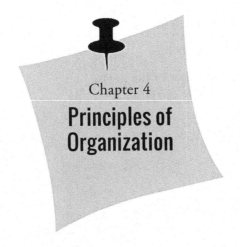

Chapter 4

Principles of Organization

"A place for everything, everything in its place."
~ Benjamin Franklin

The principles of organization are the same no matter what you're trying to do – whether it's organizing your executive's files or a stack of recipe cards. Yet organization principles still need to be tailored to fit the situation. Cleaning your desk is going to require a slightly different approach than organizing your email inbox. However, the basic steps are the same.

4 Basic Steps to Organizing Anything

I've learned a lot from professional organizers throughout the years, and this four-step organization process is one of the most valuable I have come across. It's simple, and it's applicable to just about every situation.

1. Gather similar items together.

2. Contain the items.

3. Label the items.

4. Create a home for the items.

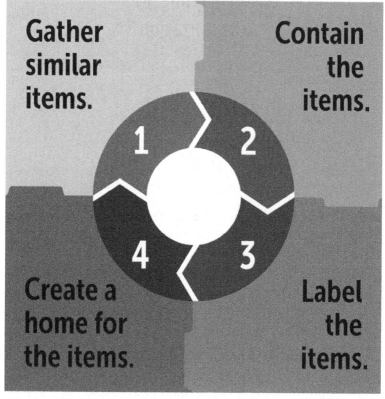

Gather similar items.

Contain the items.

Create a home for the items.

Label the items.

1

2

3

4

© Julie Perrine International, LLC

Here's how to apply these four principles to a few office organization scenarios:

Organizing office supplies on your desk

1. Gather all office supplies that are on and around your desk.

2. Find a tray, box, or desktop sorter to put them in. Some items may simply need to be put away if they already have a home in a drawer or cupboard.

3. Label the container so you (and those around you) know what goes in it.

4. Find a permanent home for this container on your desktop or in a nearby drawer or cupboard.

Organizing papers on your desk

1. Gather all of your papers together. Sort them into stacks by category or topic.

2. Contain the stacks by using file folders or expanding files. You may also need to use binder clips, paper clips, or staples to contain the groupings of paperwork in each file folder.

3. Label the file folders with the name of the contents.

4. Create a home for each file in a file drawer or desktop file sorter.

Organizing digital files

(Note: These are the same basic steps, but the terminology is slightly different.)

1. Gather all of your files into one online folder or shared drive.

2. Identify the broad categories of file types (e.g., projects, forms, travel planning, event planning, reports, executive A, executive B). This is the digital equivalent of creating containers for your files.

3. Create folders for each category. This is your digital label. You may also need to create subfolders if your main folder size gets too big.

4. Move files into their respective folders. This is the new home for each file.

If you have a lot of projects or specific types of events that require additional subfolders, you can create them to continue adding organization to your digital files.

Keep Organizing Simple

Once you have the basic organization principles down, I recommend gathering a few key office supplies to make the organizing process more seamless, including:

- 1 box of hanging file folders – letter size

- 1 box of manila file folders – 1/3 cut, letter size

- 1 box of colored file folders – 1/3 cut, letter size

- 3-4 pads of assorted color sticky notes – 3" square size

- 2 pencils

- 2 pens (blue or black)

- 2 black permanent markers (fine or bullet tip)

- 1 file folder box or plastic tub designed for hanging files
- 1 box of clear, quart-size storage bags that zip close
- 1 box of clear, gallon-size storage bags that zip close
- 1 package of mailing address labels (optional)

Having these basics at your fingertips will make it easier for you to gather, contain, label, and create homes for things quickly. You're much more likely to put something in a file folder and label it if the tools you need are easily accessible.

I recommend keeping empty file folders and hanging files within an arm's reach of where you sit. The file folder box or plastic tub makes the filing and sorting process easier because it's portable and accessible on your desktop or beside your chair. And the clear, zip-top storage bags are easy to label and keeps things tidy and contained – even in areas where you have limited storage available.

Organization Doesn't Mean Perfection

Perfection hinders a lot of admins when it comes to creating the labels for files and containers around the office.

You might think your file folder tabs have to be perfectly printed labels, so you wait until you have time to create the beautiful labels. But this only adds to the clutter and disorganization on our desk. A handwritten file folder tab still identifies and organizes the information, so you – or anyone you work with – can find it.

This is the point of organizing in the first place. When there's a massive stack of paper on your desk, it's not organized, useful, or easy to locate for anyone. You can always come back and create the nicely formatted labels later, but for now, simply get the papers gathered, contained, labeled, and placed in their rightful home.

To get and stay organized, you have to put these basic principles to use and put things back in their place when you're done using them. It really is that simple. If something doesn't have a home, create one. If it does have a home, put it away. Follow the old adage, "A place for everything, everything in its place."

PLAN OF ACTION:

☐ Gather the office supplies you'll need to get started organizing.

   ☐ 1 box of hanging file folders – letter size

   ☐ 1 box of manila file folders – 1/3 cut, letter size

   ☐ 1 box of colored file folders – 1/3 cut, letter size

   ☐ 3-4 pads of assorted color sticky notes – 3" square size

   ☐ 2 pencils

   ☐ 2 pens (blue or black)

   ☐ 2 black permanent markers (fine or bullet tip)

   ☐ 1 file folder box or plastic tub designed for hanging files

   ☐ 1 box of clear, quart-size food storage bags that zip close

☐ 1 box of clear, gallon-size food storage bags that zip close

☐ 1 package of mailing address labels (optional)

☐ Identify one section on your desk or office where you can apply the four principles of organizing outlined in this chapter. Take a picture of the area before you begin organizing it.

☐ Gather, contain, label, and create a home for those items.

☐ Time yourself. How long did the entire process take you? Write it down in your organization journal. How did you feel when you were finished? Take a picture of the area when you are finished.

☐ Repeat these steps until all areas of your desk or office area have a home.

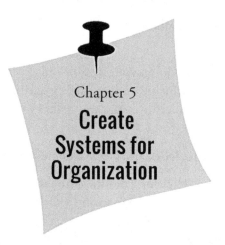

Chapter 5

Create Systems for Organization

"The true test of an ultimate assistant is how things run when s/he is not there. The most organized assistants are not the only people who know the password or have the key or know where the files are. One never knows when that proverbial bus is going to hit us, and the need to be ready has never been more obvious."
~ BONNIE LOW-KRAMEN, BESTSELLING
AUTHOR OF *BE THE ULTIMATE ASSISTANT*,
INTERNATIONAL SPEAKER & TRAINER

I define organization as the process of creating systems to find, do, or complete things. So let's look more closely at the nuts and bolts of good systems that will provide a foundation for helping you be more organized.

What Are Systems?

Systems are an ordered and proven process that save you time, effort, and unnecessary stress. They are a set of instructions that create structure or govern actions. They make behaviors automatic so you don't have to think about it. Systems have a start and a finish. They are documentable, sharable, and repeatable – so they help you deliver the same results over and over again.

Systems are at the heart of success as an administrative professional because they enable you to provide consistent service, gain credibility, establish trust, and build confidence with those you support. Systems are also key in navigating change – both expected and unexpected – and help you course-correct more adeptly. They allow you to create calm out of chaos. They can also provide great relief when someone else has to fill in for you.

Ultimately, systems allow you to create an office that functions smoothly, efficiently, and effectively…no matter what happens.

What Types of Systems Do You Need?

We need systems in all areas of our personal and professional lives. I have personal systems for managing my health and wellness, self-care, friendships, home management, and more. On the professional side, I have systems managing my career, professional network, and the day-to-day operations of my office.

Some systems we employ to keep things running smoothly are so habitual that we don't realize a system is being used. However, for the areas that may not be running so smoothly, it's an opportunity to strategize what you're doing, what's working, what isn't working, and the changes you need to make.

How Do You Create Effective Systems?

Creating systems is as simple as putting pen to paper. Good systems are documentable, so you start by writing down the process required to accomplish the task at hand. A system can be as simple as a checklist or as complex as an instruction manual.

Once you document your system, test it. That's the best way to make sure you've captured all of the details necessary. Better yet, have someone else test it. If they can successfully complete the process outlined, you're all set.

The final step is to make sure your documented systems and procedures are easily accessible. They need to be easy to review, update, and share with others. You don't want multiple copies stored across multiple drives or shared folders. You need one central location where you can share access for those who need them.

Now that you understand the purpose of systems, let's dive deeper and look at the main components of systems: templates, forms, checklists, and procedures.

What Is a Template?

A template is a format for a document or file that you set up so you can use it again and again. If you have a digital letterhead, memorandum, presentation slides, standard report, or meeting agenda that you regularly use, it's probably set up as a template. With a template, you can quickly and easily create new documents based on the template because it contains all of the formatting, fonts, headers, footers, layouts, and style elements you need.

What Is a Form?

Forms create a logical and orderly flow to information that needs to be collected or shared with others. A form is typically a document with blank spaces for information to be inserted – either electronically or in print. Think about all of the information you need to collect for a task or project. Then capture and organize it in a logical way so you're able to efficiently get the right information when you need it.

What Is a Checklist?

A checklist is a list of things, such as things to do or materials required for a job, that helps you remember all of the details you tend to forget. Checklists are usually created with small checkboxes down the left-hand side of a page and a logical order to the information on the list.

Admins have been using checklists for years, but are you using them enough? You might think, "Oh, that's not that important" or "I'll remember that." Stop. Get the details on paper. Place the paper in your procedures binder. And stop trying to remember all of this stuff. You need to clear that headspace for more important things, like coming up with innovative solutions to challenges, and thinking about what you're doing and why.

I created one of my favorite checklists after I forgot to make car service arrangements for my executive. I didn't realize it until he was headed out the door. It was almost too late. The panic and stress of that situation helped me develop one of the most comprehensive checklists for travel planning. It's four pages long, and I haven't forgotten an important travel detail for my executives since I created it.

What Is a Procedure?

Procedures are a documented way of doing things. They provide a backup plan for someone covering for you during an absence, and they help you remember the step-by-step process for daily responsibilities.

Procedures are also a great tool for helping you overcome interruptions and getting back into a focused state quickly when the interruption goes away. They can make it easier to take a big task and break it down into smaller, achievable stages.

Let me share an example. I was coaching an admin named Laura who was responsible for entering contracts into her company's contract management system. The system had several different areas where things had to be cross-referenced or double-checked before completing the upload of a new contract. It required a good memory and a lot of focus to get a single contract entered. Laura had interruptions coming at her all day, so she often struggled with getting the project started. As a result, contracts were piling up on her desk, and her team didn't have access to the most current information in the contract management system, causing them to not trust their system.

During a coaching call, I asked Laura to take me through the process from start to finish, and I documented it on paper. It took us approximately 20 minutes as Laura tried to complete each step from memory. On our next call, Laura did the procedure from start to finish following the written procedure step-by-step on paper as I observed. It took her 10 minutes. That's the value and time savings of procedures – even for everyday tasks!

We didn't stop there either. As we looked at Laura's procedure on paper, there were some natural breaks in the process that would allow us to batch certain steps and save even more time. The first batch included scanning all of the contracts, emailing them to her inbox, and saving them to a shared drive folder. The second batch of steps included uploading each file to a program that would do an optical character reading conversion so the file contents could be read by the contract management system. The third batch of steps involved saving the files to the correct location within the contract management system, tagging them with the appropriate details, and saving them.

Once we identified the full procedure and broke it down into batches, it made it much easier to do it in smaller chunks of time. It also made it more efficient because we were saving time by batching steps instead of going from start to finish on each individual contract she touched.

 File Download: If you don't know where to start, use the procedures template available at **TheOrganizedAdmin.com**. This template has helped hundreds of assistants get started documenting their office procedures and the systems they use to effectively do their jobs.

Converting Files into Forms, Templates, Checklists, and Procedures

What are the repetitive things you do each day, week, or year? You can save yourself a lot of time and stress by converting them into forms, checklists, or templates. Files on travel planning, event planning, webinar/meeting planning, and monthly reports are all great candidates.

For an event planning form, include all details you typically need to know to plan an event. For a travel planning form, include sections for private charter/commercial flights, ground transportation, hotel, meals, etc.

What information do you wish your executives or colleagues would provide up front to make your job easier? Turn it into a form or checklist!

I've used the same forms, templates, checklists, and procedures concepts at every job I've ever held. I always adjust and modify them to fit the new situation, but the principles are still as effective today as they were 20 years ago.

The following are some ways that templates, forms, checklists, and procedures can help you get organized and stay organized at the office:

- **Remember important details.** Your brain is only capable of remembering three to four important chunks of information at the same time, which makes a checklist or two or three very helpful. It ensures you remember all of the important, but not critical, things that you are responsible for each day.

- **Capture the correct information immediately.** Has your executive ever walked up to your desk and started doing a brain dump on travel arrangements they need made? When you have a form for this, you can start capturing the important information immediately. You'll also likely get more of what you need because you have a trigger in front of you on what else you need to ask your executive.

- **Visual cues and reminders.** I've used checklists for start-of and end-of-the-day tasks that someone would need to do if they were covering for me. But some days you might need the visual reminder for yourself to do tasks like unforwarding the phones or unlocking the front door of your office.

- **Switch-tasking facilitator.** As admins, we often try to multitask, but it's not always productive. The brain has to switch quickly back and forth between tasks. Checklists, forms, templates, and procedures help you switch back and forth between tasks much more quickly and efficiently.

- **Office absences.** Finally, the templates, forms, and checklists you create become great procedures for others to follow if someone needs to cover for you. Then you and your executive don't have to worry about who is covering for you because you both know the systems are in place to make sure things run smoothly.

Templates, forms, checklists, and procedures are all very similar, but each has its own unique purpose in helping us be more organized. Just remember: Templates keep us consistent. Forms keep us prepared. Checklists help us remember all of the details we tend to forget. Procedures provide the system for how to get things done.

PLAN OF ACTION:

☐ Identify one area of your daily responsibilities where a template, form, checklist, or procedure would help you better manage the project or task.

☐ Do a brain dump of all of the details that go into completing that project or task.

☐ Start organizing the details in order of importance or completion.

☐ Leave blank lines next to items to indicate information that needs to be collected each time you do this project or task.

☐ Leave check boxes next to items you need to check off as having completed each time you do this project or task.

☐ Number the items that must be done in a specific order.

☐ Use a bulleted list for items that are not order-specific to make it easy to read.

☐ Test out your template, form, checklist, or procedure. Update it after you use it a few times to perfect it for ongoing use.

☐ Repeat this process to create a system for each project or task you are responsible for.

Part 2: Organizing Ideas, Time, and Space

With the basic principles of organization in mind, it's time to apply them to these core areas:

- Organizing Your Ideas

- Workspace Organization

- Paper and Digital Filing Organization

- Organizing Your Time: To-Do Lists, Tasks, and Calendar Management

Chapter 6

Organizing Your Ideas

"Ideas are fleeting; they must be captured. I find that some of the biggest payoffs from thinking occur when I record my thoughts."
~ MARK SANBORN, LEADERSHIP EXPERT
AND BEST-SELLING AUTHOR

Keeping physical items organized is a big challenge for a lot of admins. But what can be even more difficult is keeping intangibles, such as thoughts and ideas, organized. However, it's not impossible if you can teach yourself one very important skill: journaling.

When most people think about journaling, it conjures up memories of homework assignments made by grade school teachers. But that's not what we're talking about.

In its simplest form, a journal is a place to capture ideas, record activities, and work through your thoughts, feelings, and experiences. It helps you answer questions about what's going on in your life and why. It's a means for tracking your professional accomplishments and failures. It provides a productive outlet for venting about how you feel. And it's a powerful organization tool that can help you think better and smarter.

When it comes to getting organized, writing about the areas you struggle with the most can help you productively identify and work through the challenge spots with more success. Yet starting and keeping a journal can be difficult. It's hard to find time in an already busy schedule for one more thing. But it's a little easier if you have a plan and the right tools for incorporating journaling into your life.

Journaling Methods

There's no right or wrong way to keep a journal. This isn't a research paper that you're going to be graded on. You don't even have to use complete sentences if you don't want to. You can journal by drawing, jotting down quick lists, or writing. You can cut things out and tape them into your journal. You can journal with photos, audio, and/or video. You can use small notepads or large sketchbooks. You can use apps and smartphones. Or you can do any combination of the above.

What's important is that the method works well for you, and it's something that you'll stick with. You may need to try several methods before you settle into the one that fits your personality type and organizing preferences.

Journaling Options

Think about how you typically capture notes or ideas. Is it with pen and paper, digitally, or a combination of the two? The answer to that question will help you identify the journaling tool(s) you may want to try.

Some people prefer paper; some prefer digital methods. I actually recommend a system that includes both so you can capture things quickly – whether you're online or offline. You can use your electronic devices to capture ideas, but there is something about physically writing and the journaling process that you may miss if you just use digital tools to capture your thoughts. Sometimes you may need space to doodle and draw to maximize your creative moments. Other times you may need the speed and efficiency of an electronic tool. That's why I strongly recommend a combination of journaling methods to maximize your time and energy.

Here are some things to consider as you look at the three options for journaling:

1. **Paper.** Whether it's an actual journal, themed notebook, leather planner, or binder with lined paper, there's no wrong choice. If you like to write your notes and thoughts down, instead of type them, a paper journal is the way to go. Plus, this option gives you the ability to draw or diagram if you need to visually flesh out your thoughts.

2. **Digital.** Type up your journal entries in a word processing program, or use a note-capturing app or program. You can even use a video or audio app to keep your journal! This option is ideal if you want your journal to be a bit more portable and accessible from anywhere and on multiple devices.

3. **A combo of paper and digital.** If you choose a combination approach, make sure you create a home for storing

your various journals so you can access them quickly and conveniently when you want to capture an idea or make an entry.

It's OK to test several methods before you settle on your custom journaling system. Give each one a try. Write down your thoughts on what you like or dislike about each method you test. After a couple weeks, evaluate how it's working. Then tailor your system to whatever works best for you and inspires you to journal. You need to get the right method – otherwise you're less likely to stick with journaling.

Regardless of whether you choose paper, digital, or both for your normal journaling, I encourage you to carry a portable paper journal that fits in a pocket or small handbag so you can jot down ideas as they come to you. That way you're always prepared when an idea or thought needs to be captured.

 What I Use: Visit **TheOrganizedAdmin.com** to view examples of various types of journaling systems I have used.

Capturing Your Thoughts and Ideas

Once you choose your journal method, it's fairly easy to start getting your thoughts and ideas documented. When you get an idea that you want to pursue, capture it! When you see a product, tool, or website, or have an idea that you want to research, save it to your digital journal. Install a web clipper add-on to your web browser so it's quick and easy to capture ideas when you're online. If you find a resource you want to come back to later, write it down. Documenting ideas and interesting tidbits you find throughout the day becomes a great tool to help get the creative juices flowing and innovative solutions brewing.

Don't think too rigidly about journaling. It can be an art form all its own! You can use a journal to keep track of whatever you want – the important thing is to use it to create a capture system for keeping your thoughts, ideas, and insights organized in some way. Some things to journal about include:

- Lists

- Ideas

- To-dos

- Accomplishments of the day or week

- Failures

- Problems you're trying to solve

- Things you're thankful for

- Significant life events

- Things you're learning

- Things you want to learn

- Goals progress and tracking

- Anything you feel like writing down

With your thoughts and ideas captured, you can continue adding to them. You can also use your journal as a tool for working through how to turn those thoughts and ideas into something you can implement. A lot of people have good ideas that never get implemented because they forgot about them, or didn't have a productive way to work through the steps to make it happen.

Implementation is one of the most important and challenging parts of developing your capacity for innovation. You can't generate ideas, not execute them, and expect to stand out and get noticed. You have to implement. You can't implement without a plan. And you can't plan without paper or a good digital mapping tool. This is why journaling is such a valuable and important skill to develop – not just for being organized, but also for advancing your admin career!

The Benefits of Journaling

Journaling helps you de-clutter and organize your mind. It applies the four principles of organization to the intangible by creating a place for you to gather, sort, label, and contain your ideas and thoughts. It takes all of the things that are floating around in your head and gives them a permanent place to live until you're ready to retrieve them and take action. And the relief you feel knowing you won't forget something – because you'll be referring back to your journal – is a wonderful feeling.

As a busy admin, you might be wondering, "How can I fit in journaling when I am already working five days a week with little time to spare?" The important thing to remember is that journaling helps you be more organized, which in turn will make you more efficient and productive and free up more time and head space.

However, these aren't the only perks to getting yourself organized with a journal.

- **Journaling can help you reduce stress.** Much of the stress we feel stems from work. Stress can lead to sickness and underperformance, so anything that reduces stress is good. Using a journal to organize your thoughts is an excellent way to do this. Getting stressful thoughts, such as tasks or to-dos, out of your head is cathartic and alleviates the need to remember them. So you just have to remember one thing – to look at your journal – instead of several things.

- **Journaling can help you become a better problem solver.** By documenting the pros and cons of a work-related problem, you map it all out on paper, meaning you can view it from a clearer, fresher perspective. This typically makes it easier for you to analyze all your options more clearly and come up with a better solution. It can also help you generate new ideas and explore how to implement them.

- **Journaling can help you grow personally and professionally.** Journaling can help personal growth by allowing you to better understand your work and life experiences. You can express yourself in your journal without fear of judgment. It will help you to take a step back and take more of a bird's-eye view of how you handle these experiences so that you can explore, understand, and learn from your work experiences. Journaling is a great tool for helping you create, track, and measure your progress on annual performance goals, too. It is this overall process of personal reflection that can help you grow as a person, ultimately making you more effective in the workplace.

Tips on Journaling

Are you ready to use journaling to improve your organization? Before you begin, I highly recommend you take a look at some of my journaling best practices. They will help keep you engaged and committed to your journaling efforts.

- Most people have better results when they journal on a daily basis, perhaps even at a specific time of the day. But the key is to remain flexible. If you miss a day, or your set window of journaling time, pick it back up the next day. Remember: No one is grading you on this!

- Date your journal entries. It's easy to forget when things occurred, and having dates on your journal entries will help you recall events and details more accurately.

- Journaling doesn't have to involve hours of writing; it can be as quick and simple as spending 60 seconds recording a quick video or audio, creating a list, jotting down some random thoughts, drawing a picture, or making notes so you remember to journal more on a specific topic later. This still helps you clear your head and process information in a productive manner.

- If possible, when it's time to work on your journal, retreat to a quiet place where you can be alone with your thoughts and won't be distracted.

Think of a journal as your own unique art form. Nobody is going to grade you on your journal. You don't need to share it with anyone else. You just need to follow these steps, start writing, and transform your ideas into action items. Use these guidelines to create a nurturing environment for your journaling and start working on yours today!

PLAN OF ACTION:

☐ Purchase a regular journal and a smaller journal or notepad for when you're on the go. Commit to carrying the smaller journal with you all of the time.

☐ Set up an online folder or install an applicable software program where you can capture ideas when you are on your computer or electronic devices throughout the day.

☐ Create your first journal entry using the ideas listed in this chapter.

☐ Commit to writing in your regular journal at least once a week – but daily updating is encouraged.

Chapter 7

Workspace Organization

*"Your goal needn't be to have empty surfaces,
but to have a place for everything."*
~ KACY PAIDE, OFFICE ORGANIZING
EXPERT, THEINSPIREDOFFICE.COM

As an admin, it's your job to keep tabs on everything your executive and others you support need to do their jobs. For you to be successful in this responsibility, you need to be able to quickly and easily locate files, information, and other materials. This requires organization on various levels, and one of the most important is your workspace.

Workspace organization can be a process, especially if yours looks like a tornado blew through it. A messy, unorganized desk not only makes it difficult for you to find things, it reflects poorly on your level of professionalism and credibility as an admin. Even if you can find what you need amid the chaos, those who pass by your desk may walk away with a perception of your skills and competence level that isn't accurate because of how your workspace looks.

Let's look at a few ideas for helping you get your desk, files, and workspace in order.

Eliminate Clutter

One of the biggest visual upgrades you can make in your workspace is to remove nonessential things. Clutter accumulates when things don't have a home or don't get put away, and you don't make a decision about what to do with things. If you look around your workspace and see a lot of clutter, here's a quick way to remedy it:

1. Take absolutely everything off of your desk. Throw trash items and dead plants away. Put everything else in a box.

2. Determine which items are essential to your daily work, and place them back on your desk. Or better yet, find a desk drawer (a home) where they can live.

3. Leave the other items in the box and place it under or near your desk. Keep it there for at least a month. Store or get rid of any items in the box that you don't use during that time. If you have personal items you want to keep, such as family photos, consider reducing the quantity or placing them outside of your primary work zone to reduce the visual clutter.

Once you've tackled the top of your desk, move on to getting rid of the clutter in your desk drawers, including your junk drawer, using these same three steps. If you feel overwhelmed tackling all the drawers at once, simply work on one at a time. Also remove the clutter from around your desk by emptying your shred bin, recycle bin, and other trash. Throw dead plants away or prune them back to a healthier state.

Clearing the clutter creates a refreshed environment that will help you work more efficiently and think more clearly. You'll be amazed at how calming a clean workspace is for you and those who come to your desk.

Establish Work Zones

With the clutter cleared, it's time to think about your workspace in terms of how you use it. Then you need to establish three primary zones.

Zone one is your prime real estate. This is the main workspace at your desk – the center of activity that is within arm's reach of your computer and phone. This is where you put things you use and access consistently throughout the day as you work. This area is also for current projects you are working on. I encourage you to remove items, such as personal photos and trinkets, from this zone so you can maintain focus and reserve this zone for the important items that help you work efficiently.

Zone two is where you stage your work for the day. This is the area immediately next to zone one with your active project folders, incoming-mail tray, and the things you need easily accessible as you work on your active projects. If you find comfort in having a personal photo or two on your desk, this zone is the better place for those items.

Zone three is for storage, archives, and supplies. These are the things you rarely touch during the day, but need to be able to access them when needed. Zone three is ideal for the personal items you bring with you to the office, such as your coat, lunch, or work-out gear, so it doesn't take up space in your primary work zones.

Work From Left to Right

With zones established, it's easier to organize how work flows across your desk. This is a challenge a lot of admins face. Some projects can be completed from start to finish the first time you touch them. Others have to be worked through in stages. New things are added daily, so it's easy to end up with piles of important files and papers accumulating around you. And if you aren't careful, it can become unsightly and disorganized very quickly.

To remedy this, work from left to right. Start the day with your to-do stack on the left side of your desk. As you complete tasks or projects, move them to the right side. Or put tasks in a pending stack while you wait for feedback or follow-up. This will help you keep track of your progress and what still needs to be done at the end of the day. You might have to reorganize your desk to make this work, but it's worth it to have a consistent workflow for projects.

Working from left to right also has a side benefit in that it gives you a visual cue as to where you are with the day's priority list. This can be especially helpful if more is added to your list and you need help prioritizing things you still have to accomplish. At the end of the day, when you're planning for the next day, you'll be able to quickly identify what's done, what's pending, and what still needs to be addressed.

Color-Code Everything

Another way to add structure and organization to your workspace is to use color-coding. Assign a different color to each executive, team, or project you support. Then use the appropriate color for corresponding file folders, labels, and even your calendar and tasks. Color-coding will help you find things quickly and keep everything visually consistent in your workspace. Plus, if you're out of the office and someone is looking for a file, it's a lot easier to direct the person to it if you can say, "Look for the orange files."

Showcase Your Incoming-Mail Tray

You don't need to put a spotlight on it, but your incoming-mail tray should be very obvious and easy to find. Make sure it's in a highly visible spot on your desk to ensure your executive and colleagues can locate it. Then make a habit of emptying it every day. If your co-workers don't think you're handling the items in your inbox, they'll start placing them in other spots on your desk or chair. This creates more clutter and the potential for important papers to get overlooked.

Get a Keyboard Tray or Hide Your Keyboard

One easy way to add more space to your work area is to hide or relocate your keyboard. If you don't have a keyboard tray, I highly recommend you get one. If that's not possible, put your laptop or monitor on a riser or stand that's wide enough to accommodate your keyboard. Both of these options will give you a place to put your keyboard when you're not typing/using your computer, and make more room on your desk.

File as You Go

I know filing as you go sounds great in theory. But for most admins, it usually fails in practice. The reason it fails is because the right supplies for creating and labeling aren't within reach. So files get tossed into that black hole known as the "file pile" and it plagues us mentally for days and weeks to come. That's no way to work.

You can easily file as you go when you have the tools you need easily accessible. Take a couple of minutes to create a filing supply station on your desk or at the front of a file drawer. Include marking pens, labels, an assortment of plain and colored file folders, and hanging files that coordinate with your color-coding system. Then sort and label the papers, files, etc. that land on your desk. Create files as you need them, and file the items once or twice throughout the day. If you know that filing typically takes you 15 minutes a day or 30 minutes a week, then schedule the time on your calendar each day or week to get it done.

You don't need perfectly printed labels to file something either. A handwritten file tab is still a labeled and contained location for your papers that can still be easily located.

Workspace Organization Tools

Now that you have some strategies and tools to create a tidier and organized workspace, it's time for my favorite part of organizing: office supply shopping!

I love shopping for office supplies, especially ones that will keep me organized. However, if it's not something you enjoy, you can always rely on an office supply catalog or online provider. Regardless of how you get your supplies, these are some that I highly recommend putting in your cart:

- All-in-one desk organizers. These are great for keeping sticky notes, tape flags, pens, clips, tape, staplers, etc., organized and within reach on your desk.

- Divided trays for your desk drawers.

- Hanging files and interior files.

- Poly pockets.

- Labeler.

- A stapler, staple remover, clips, pens, and a container to keep them all in. The container and its contents should go next to the office copier.

- Expandable files for projects that need to be portable.

- Projects tubs with lockable lids and handles. These make it easy to tote files to and from meetings or file storage areas away from your desk.

- Smead Viewables filing software and supplies.

- Assorted colors and sizes of three-ring binders.

I encourage you to start your shopping trip at the office supply drawer or cabinet in your office. There's no need to buy new items when you already have them in stock. You may not need all of these items either. But buying a few will help you contain, label, and create permanent homes for the clutter and papers that are littering your workspace. They're also the perfect solution to keeping your desk chaos-free once it's organized.

To maintain your clean workspace, you may need to teach colleagues where they need to put incoming mail, project requests, and other materials they bring to your desk. You may also need to schedule 10-15 minutes each day to do a triage if things tend to get out of control. Dedicating this time will help you regain any lost ground more quickly than waiting until the end of the week. Developing this new habit and utilizing workspace organization tools will not only make your feel better, it will help you be more productive, too!

Reclaiming Your Desk After an Absence

When you work hard at maintaining a tidy and organized workspace, it's disheartening to return from an absence to find things in total disarray. While it may take you a day or two to bring order back, good organization systems and the basic organization principles we've outlined will make it easier to regain the lost ground. You can also do a few other things to make reclaiming your desk easier:

- Place a sign on your computer monitor stating that you'll be out of the office from this date to that date. Include a contact name and number of someone they can contact in your absence. Just make sure the person you're referring people to knows they're the contact point. In the event of an unscheduled absence, you may want to have a generic sign ready for a colleague to place on your desk.

- Create an office procedures binder so others can fill in for you. If someone can follow your procedures for getting routine tasks done, it will keep them from piling up while you're out.

- Place clearly labeled bins or trays on your desk during your absence so people know where to place certain items such as incoming mail, assignments, supply deliveries, etc. You may need to put specific names on the bins so you can quickly triage requests or files from key people you work with.

- Allow time for reclaiming your desk when you return. This may mean coming in a little early, staying a little late, or blocking off a couple of hours so you have time to process through things.

Just as your attire is a key in how people form a first impression of your skills and abilities, your workspace also makes an impression. When someone enters your office and sees your desk, what will they think? Take a picture of your desk and work space from the other side of your desk. What do you see when you look at it from a different angle?

Apply the strategies I've outlined in this chapter to refresh and declutter your work space. Give your desk an organization makeover. It will positively impact your productivity and the first impressions you make every day.

PLAN OF ACTION:

☐ Take before pictures of your workspace, desk drawers, file drawers, and storage cabinets in your immediate work area.

☐ Take a picture of your desk and work space from the other side of your desk. What do you notice most about your work area when you look at it from a different perspective? (Tip: After you get it organized, take another picture and compare.)

☐ Clear the clutter from your desk.

   ☐ Take absolutely everything off your desk. Throw trash items and dead plants away and put everything else in a box.

   ☐ Determine which items are essential to your daily work, and put them back on your desk. Or find a desk drawer (a home) where they can live.

   ☐ Leave the other items in the box and place it under or near your desk. Keep it there for at least a month. If you don't need those items in that time, you can probably store or get rid of them. If you have personal items you want to keep, such as family photos, consider reducing the quantity or placing them outside of your primary work zone to reduce the visual clutter.

☐ Empty your junk drawer.

   ☐ Remove all of the items from your junk drawer and place them in a box.

   ☐ Throw away any items that are trash.

   ☐ Find a desk tray, sorter, or a couple small boxes to place in the drawer.

   ☐ Determine which items are essential to your daily work, group them with like items, and place them back in the desk drawer.

☐ Review what's left in the box. Place extra supplies in the supply cabinet. Create files for important paperwork. Get rid of anything you no longer need.

☐ Showcase your incoming-mail tray. Create an incoming-mail sign so it's visible for everyone who comes to your desk.

☐ Create or document your color-coding system for files and projects.

☐ Order any office supplies you need to set up your filing station and workspace.

☐ Take after pictures of your workspace, desk drawers, file drawers, and storage cabinets in your immediate work area. Compare them to the before pictures and congratulate yourself on your progress!

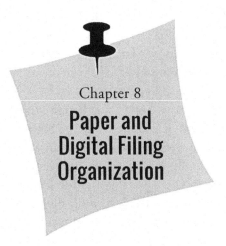

Chapter 8

Paper and Digital Filing Organization

"The only way around is through."
~ ROBERT FROST

The infamous to-file pile. Do you have one? When was the last time you made time to catch up on your filing?

I used to have a to-file pile. In fact, I didn't just have a pile…I had a labeled tray for it. And that tray gave me permission to procrastinate. So I did. I would have to dig through that pile countless times in a week to find something because I hadn't filed it yet. That pile just kept growing until I eventually had to spend several hours labeling things and putting them in their proper place. It was complete craziness.

My to-file tray wasn't helping me stay organized at all. In fact, it was depressing me every time I looked at it. So I examined why I was resisting filing in the first place. My findings were key in helping me permanently eliminate the to-file habit.

One big reason I resisted filing – and I suspect I'm not alone – was because I had this notion that the labels for my file folder tabs needed to be typed before I could put something in a file or store it in a file drawer. This was far from the truth. The purpose of a file folder is to contain and label similar items so you can then store everything in its rightful place.

Another reason I struggled was because filing was inconvenient to do on the spot and took way too long. I didn't have the tools or supplies I needed to quickly grab a folder and create a label. Filing usually means getting up from your desk, walking to a supply cabinet, locating the file folders, walking back to your desk, printing a label, feeding the label sheet into the printer, retrieving the label from the printer, and finally assembling your file. It's no wonder we resist filing! The process needs to be simple.

I went from spending hours catching up on my filing to taking just a couple minutes each day to do. How did I do it? I applied a few simple fixes, which I'll share with you in this chapter.

When it comes to filing, there are two basic categories to address: paper and digital. To keep your filing system as organized as possible, it helps if the structures of your paper and electronic files mirror one another. This helps you think more clearly about where things are placed and how to find them again later.

Before You Begin Filing

One of the questions you have to ask yourself about the papers and files laying around is should you be saving them in the first place? A lot of the paper that accumulates on our desks is redundant and outdated by the time we get around to doing something with it. If it doesn't need to be saved or you have it electronically, trash it or shred it. If it's something you can scan and save digitally, do it. (We'll talk more about keeping your digital files organized later in this chapter.) Legal documents and financial files may require you to store the originals. If you aren't sure what's important to save and what can be tossed, ask your executive, check with legal and accounting, and consult with human resources. They should be able to provide guidance in these areas.

Once you purge and prioritize the remaining paper on your desk, here are some strategies for organizing it more effectively.

Categorizing Files

Before you tackle your to-file pile, you need to create some structure to follow. If your filing system is random and unorganized, start by identifying the categories or groupings for your files. You may have categories such as: Accounting, Legal, Marketing, Operations, Projects, etc.

Once you identify your major categories, break them down into smaller, logical groups or subcategories. For example, your Operations pile may have subcategories such as:

- Building Lease

- Copier Repair & Maintenance

- Parking Permit Administration

- Employee Badges & Keys

Less is more when you are just starting to create subcategories, so don't go crazy creating them if you don't actually need them. If your primary file is starting to get too full, then it's probably time to break it down into additional files.

Develop a Color Code

Color-coding applies more to paper files than digital files. However, many programs and task management tools allow you to add category colors so you can carry them over to your digital file management too.

If you don't have the budget or approval to use colored file folders, you can still use color on your labels or apply colored stickers to make them more visual. Color can make a world of difference in quickly finding things or identifying when something is misplaced. Depending on how many colors and categories you create, it may be helpful to you (and those you support) to create a color code key. That way everyone knows the system, and you have a better chance of maintaining it.

Here are some color-coding examples I've used and my methodology behind them:

- Project Types

  ○ Business development projects are green (for money)

  ○ Administrative projects are blue (for corporate)

  ○ Speaking projects are red (for hot item or important)

- Executives – I always assign a color to each executive I support. Then I have three, 1/3 cut folders labeled in their color for ongoing use:

  ○ Executive's Name – Signature File

  ○ Executive's Name – Meeting/Travel Planning

  ○ Executive's Name – Projects (or Open Items)

Organize Paper Files

Keeping paper files organized can be trickier than organizing digital ones because they require a physical home. So it's important to implement some strategies and tools to ensure you stay on top of your filing and get everything in its rightful place.

Create a File-on-the-Go Station

To make filing a seamless task that's as much a part of your day as answering the phone and greeting guests, you need all of the vital tools for filing at your fingertips. Find a free-standing, vertical tray sorter with one or two sections. Place the sorter on your desk within arm's reach of where you sit at your computer. Stock it with an assortment of file folders you use. Mine includes a combination of 1/3 cut manila folders, an assortment of 1/3 cut color folders, and a variety of poly folders that I use for organizing my projects. You may also want to include a good writing pen, marker, or pencil for labeling your folders.

Label Your Files

You don't need a beautifully printed label to label a file. Handwritten labels work just fine. The goal is to identify the file. You can always print a label for it later. If you don't like your handwriting, use a pencil so you can erase it later when you have a printed label created. Just make sure you label everything from the moment you open the file folder and place contents in it.

I also recommend investing in a label printing machine and keeping it on your desktop or in an easily accessible drawer. This will help you quickly print labels and keep your files labeled.

What I Use: Visit **TheOrganizedAdmin.com** to see my favorite tools for printing, labeling, and color-coding file folders.

Use Tickler Files

If you have a lot of recurring things to manage, it might help to develop a weekly or annual tickler file system. This becomes your system for managing the day-to-day tasks and projects and is much more effective than big piles on your desk. Here are a few ways you can do this:

- **Daily/annual tickler folders:** One option for this type of tickler is to create a hanging file folder for each month of the year – January through December (12 files total). Then create a hanging file folder for each day of the month – 1 through 31 (31 files total). Put each item you need to remember in the appropriate month folder for when it needs to be handled or for when you need to be reminded to take action. At the beginning of each month, place the daily folders (1-31) behind that month's main folder. Review the items in the monthly folder and place the specific items in the appropriate day of the month it needs to be handled. This will require you to check the tickler file on a daily basis so you don't miss any important tasks or deadlines.

- **Weekly/annual tickler folders:** Another way you can create a tickler is with a weekly and annual setup. As with the first option, create a hanging file folder for each month of the year – January through December (12 files total). Then create a hanging file folder for each week of the month – Week 1, Week 2, Week 3, Week 4, and Week 5 (5 files total). Put each item in the appropriate month folder that it needs to be handled, or you need to be reminded to take action. At the beginning of each new month, place the five weekly folders behind that month's main folder and put each item in the week of the month that it needs to be handled. This will require you check the tickler file on a weekly basis so you don't miss any important tasks or deadlines.

- **Monthly tickler in print or digital format:** Not everything you need to remember may have a folder or printed notice to go with it. So it's important to have a system that keeps those things on your radar at the appropriate times throughout the month and year, too. If you're a mostly digital person, maintaining these tickler reminders in your Outlook Tasks or email program may work best. If you're a paper person, being able to print them so you can place them in your paper planner or your daily work folder may be another option. Maintaining your tickler file in a print or digital format is ideal for the monthly or annual recurring items you need to remember as part of your normal job responsibilities. This may include things like monthly staff meetings, quarterly board meeting preparations, legal reminders, membership renewals, and more. You can also add the one-time only tasks to your Outlook Tasks with start dates and due dates or type them into your monthly tickler list that you print so you don't lose track of them.

What I Use: Visit **TheOrganizedAdmin.com** to see how I set up my tickler file system.

Most successful tickler systems include a combination of a folder system and a digital or print format to keep you organized. Find the combination that works best for your organizing style and use it consistently. If you aren't used to checking the tickler file each day, you may need to add it to your morning startup checklist or add a reminder to your calendar each day until it becomes part of your new habit.

Active Files and Archive Files

An important thing to remember with your paper files is that not all files need to be readily accessible. Some need to be saved for archive purposes, but they don't need to occupy prime real estate in your most accessible file drawers.

One assistant I worked with had several old laptops and a stack of outdated training handouts occupying a prime file drawer next to her desk. With a call to her technology department, the laptops were returned to IT. After a quick review of the training handouts, she realized they were out of date and could be easily tossed. She freed up a lot of space very quickly.

The key here is to take an inventory of your space, identify the file drawers that are the easiest to access, figure out what's currently being stored there, and determine if it can be relocated to another area. Then, use the most accessible file drawers for your active files. Just make sure to store confidential files in a locked drawer.

Place the archive or reference files that do not get used regularly in areas that are farther from reach. Your archive files should still utilize the same filing system you use for your active files. However, they should live separate from your active files. This will help keep your file system more efficient and organized.

One important thing to consider when filing, especially when it comes to archiving files, is your company's policy on file retention. You don't want to get rid of something your company is legally required to hold on to. So check with your legal department and learn what you can and can't throw away. Once you know your company's policy, get rid of things you have multiple copies of and old items that are captured somewhere digitally (if allowed). These are easy ways to clean up and purge.

 What I Use: To take a peek inside my filing system, visit **TheOrganizedAdmin.com**.

Electronic Files

Just like papers on your desk can pile up, the same thing can happen with digital files. If you don't have a filing system to put things where they belong when you save them, the virtual mess can accumulate quickly. With digital files, it's a lot easier to ignore the problem because the virtual piles are out of sight on your hard drive. And technology makes it easy to search for files with keywords, so it can be tempting to not maintain your digital files. However, time is still wasted if you're hunting for files. So investing a little effort into organizing your digital files can actually make you more productive in the long run. Here's how you can get started.

Set Up Your Digital Filing Cabinet

1. **Create a single folder that contains all of your files.** This is your digital filing cabinet. Many use the My Documents folder that is set up by default on your computer. Or you can create a folder called My Filing Cabinet. In the past, I've named my folder Julie's Filing Cabinet. Now my team and I use an online storage tool, so it has become my default digital filing cabinet.

   What I Use: To see what I use for online storage, visit **TheOrganizedAdmin.com**.

2. **Create a designated folder for downloads.** When you're online and you download a file or save an image, you need a single, default location on your computer for saving these items. Many computers have a default Downloads folder already. If you know how to find it and use it when you're looking for downloaded files, great! If you don't know where it is or want it in a location that's easier to find, then create a new folder called My Downloads. If you do this, make sure you also change the default settings for your web browser so it automatically recognizes this as your default file location for downloads.

3. **Create categories that apply to the types of digital files you save.** If you need help coming up with ideas, look at your paper files and see what types of categories

you're using. Your digital files will likely need to follow suit. You may have categories such as: Accounting, Legal, Marketing, Operations, Projects, Executive A, Executive B, Personal, etc. These become your primary list of sub-folders under your main My Documents or My Filing Cabinet folder.

Once you identify your major categories, you may need to break them down into smaller subcategories or subfolders. For example, your Operations folder may have subcategories such as:

- Building Lease

- Copier Repair & Maintenance

- Parking Permit Administration

- Employee Badges & Keys

Organize Your Digital Filing Cabinet

Once your digital filing cabinet is set up and ready for use, take a look at your current list of files and begin the organizing process. These three steps are what I use to triage my digital files into a more organized structure when a digital folder becomes unwieldy:

1. **Gather all of your unorganized files and folders into one folder and start the sorting process.** If your files already have a good structure set up, you may be able to work from your existing online folder. If your files are completely out of control, I like to create a folder named Sorting Folder. This is the folder I work from as I move

and organize files into my digital file cabinet with my folder categories and subcategories.

2. **View your Sorting Folder in List view sorted in alphabetical order by file name.** Scan the file names to see if there are any file groupings that you can immediately identify based on file name. This will help you move (or delete) entire groups of files more quickly from the Sorting Folder to your filing cabinet folder. For example, let's say my Sorting Folder has 400 items in it. When I view it by file name, all of the past webinar alerts that I downloaded to add to my calendar appear together. These are already on my calendar so they can be deleted completely from my Sorting Folder.

3. **View your Sorting Folder in List or Details view grouped by file type.** This allows you to see all of your files grouped by JPG images, PDFs, DOCs, XLSes, PPTs, MP3s, etc. Depending on the operating system, I can immediately see how many GIF, JPEG, and JPG image files I have to sort into a graphics folder until I have time to sort them further. I can also see iCalendar files that I can delete if the items have already been added to my calendar. Using this view, I'm able to quickly triage dozens of files out of my Sorting Folder and into a better file folder for quicker retrieval later. It also allows me to quickly review the file types with only one or two files, such as CAB or HTM files, and put them in their proper places. The larger file categories – such as Adobe Acrobat, Word, or Excel files – will take a little longer. But using this view will help you gather, contain, label, and create a home for files

much quicker than going through each file one by one in alphabetical view.

When you're finished with the triage process, your Sorting Folder should be empty. Depending on the number of files you have to sort and triage, you may need to schedule some time on your calendar to work on this over the course of a couple days or even a couple weeks. But once you have your digital filing cabinet set up, you'll feel better every time you look for a file because you'll know exactly where to find it.

Maintain Your Digital Filing Cabinet

With your digital filing cabinet set up and your files sorted into their rightful places, here are a few additional tips to help you maintain this organized environment moving forward:

1. **Add your digital filing cabinet folder to your favorites list on File Explorer.** This makes it very quick and easy to get to your files from any file explorer window. To add a folder to your favorites, open your digital filing cabinet folder in File Explorer. Make sure the navigation pane is visible on the left side of the screen. Right-click on Favorites in the navigation pane. Choose "Add current location to Favorites."

2. **Create new folders in your digital filing cabinet as you need them.** If you aren't sure where to put something, think about how you may search for it later. What does it go with? If you were placing it into a physical folder on your desk, how would you categorize it? Then put it in the appropriate folder or create

a new subfolder in one of the categories that you've already set up.

3. **Avoid duplicating files in multiple places by creating file shortcuts instead.** If you have a file that you want to store in more than one digital location for convenience or ease in tracking it down later, don't copy it. Create a shortcut to it. For example, I have a binder cover that I use over and over again. I don't need to store it in every single project folder on my hard drive. Instead I can store it in my main folder, or in a forms and templates folder, and create a shortcut to it in the other places I want to access it.

   The shortcut is a link instead of a copy of the file. This saves you space on your computer and makes the original file easy to find. It also ensures you always have the latest version because you're looking at the same file instead of a copy of a copy somewhere else.

   To create a shortcut, right-click on the file name. Choose Create Shortcut. A shortcut file will appear with the file name followed by "- Shortcut." You can then move the shortcut to the folder where you want to store it.

   To open the main file, double-click on the shortcut, and it will open the file from its original location in your digital filing cabinet.

4. **Create an archive folder in your digital filing cabinet.** Sometimes there are digital files we'd like to clean up or delete from our primary list of folders, but it's important to maintain an archive in case you need to refer back to

them later. To do this, create a folder called Z-Archive. I put the Z followed by a dash in front of the folder name so it appears at the bottom of my file folder list. Sometimes you can get by with one archive folder. But I've found it's better to have one archive folder in each of my primary digital filing cabinet folders so I can quickly find the archived files for that category if I need them. This allows you to move old files out of your primary work folder and into the archive folder. This way your main folders don't become overrun with irrelevant files, which makes it harder to find your active files when you need them.

Find the File You Need When You Need It

It's easy to let your digital files get out of control because they aren't on your desk creating visual clutter. But every time you look for a file and it's not where it should be or you spend extra time doing keyword searches to find a file, you're wasting valuable time. Invest some time in creating order in your digital files, and you'll reap the rewards of increasing your productivity, reducing overwhelm, and knowing you can put your finger – or mouse – on a file anytime you need it!

Be Specific With Your File Names

The great part about many of the software tools we use today is the ability to create descriptive file names, as well as create tags or keywords for ease of searching later.

In the early days of word processing programs, the file name limit was eight characters with no symbols or spaces. Today, you can almost type entire sentences for a file name. While that may work, I encourage you to take a coordinated and thoughtful approach to how you name and organize your electronic files.

Naming your files is all about making them easy to retrieve again later. Think about what name you can give a file that will make it easy to find. With electronic files, you can create folder systems that mirror your paper folders to keep things organized. This helps you search for and locate your documents more efficiently. Just remember that electronic files might not always "live" in a specific folder if you send them to others for sharing or collaboration. So it's important to make sure key project names, owners, or terms are included in the file name. This will make it easy for others to identify and find in their system once it leaves your computer.

Here are a few file name examples to illustrate this:

- All Things Admin Speaking Proposal for ABC Company – Sept 20XX (Includes company name, type of proposal, who it's for, and the date)

- All Things Admin Board Meeting Agenda for Sept 20XX (Includes company name, type of meeting, type of document, and the date)

- All Things Admin Board Meeting Minutes from July 20XX (Includes company name, type of meeting, type of document, and the date)

- All Things Admin Website Project – Team Member Bios (Includes company name, type of project, specific aspect of the project)

If you receive a file with any of these names, you'll immediately be able to identify what it is and where it came from. And you'll probably even have a few clues as to what you need to do with it just by looking at the file name.

Use File-Naming Conventions

To create organization and structure in your electronic file folders, consider beginning each file name with a three- or four-letter abbreviation to categorize it. To figure out your abbreviations, think about the primary types or categories of documents that you create and write them down. Then create an abbreviation to represent that file type. For example:

FORM – Forms

LTR – Letters

MEMO – Memos

LBL – Labels

MAP – Maps

ENV – Envelopes

RPT – Reports

SIGN – Signs

BOD – Board of Directors

Keep this list and the abbreviations posted on a bulletin board or next to your computer so you can refer to it when creating or searching for files.

What's nice about this setup is that all of your file types show up together on the file directory list and then in alphabetical order by the name of the file. When I'm looking for a label template, I don't have to wonder what I named it. I immediately scroll down to the LBL file names and can find it quickly.

It's also handy if you create travel itineraries for multiple executives. Here's an example of a file-naming convention for travel itineraries:

> XXXXXX – Location – Name or Initials of Traveler
> (e.g. **073015 – Tampa FL – JLP**)

> XXXXXX – Location, Event, Name of Traveler
> (e.g. **073015 – Tampa FL Admin Conv JLP**)

When using dates in your file names, use six-digit dates so they always align in order numerically by date. If you're storing itineraries from multiple years in the same folder, you may want to start with a two- or four-digit year instead, so you can find things by the year, month, and day. Using the same sample data from above, this option looks like this:

2015 0730 – Tampa FL – JLP

It's easy to rename existing files by going to Windows Explorer and adding the prefix or format to your file names. Click on the file name once to select it. Click on the file name again (don't double-click) to open the editing box. The file name will appear in a box with your cursor at the beginning. You can rename the file, then click outside the file name box, and it's renamed.

Taking a few extra seconds to make your digital file names more specific or labeling a paper file as soon as you create it can go a long way in helping you maintain organization in your filing systems.

Officially Retire Your To-File Pile

When you create a system for your paper and digital files, then document it for both yourself and others to follow, it becomes part of how you work – instead of something you have to do at the end of the day. Before you know it, your to-file pile will be a thing of the past, and you'll be able to find what you need when you need it!

PLAN OF ACTION:

☐ Identify the primary reasons that you resist filing.

☐ Share your reasons with us at **TheOrganizedAdmin.com**.

☐ Brainstorm a list of the filing categories and subcategories for your job responsibilities.

☐ Document the color-coding system you use or create one to implement.

☐ Set up a file-on-the-go station to make filing part of your daily routine.

☐ Set up a tickler file system if you don't already have one that works for you.

☐ Brainstorm a list of file-naming conventions to use to help you find files more easily.

☐ Create your digital filing cabinet.

☐ Organize your digital files into the new folders in your digital filing cabinet and purge the files you no longer need as you go.

Chapter 9

Organizing Your Time: To-Do Lists, Tasks, and Calendar Management

"Every minute you spend in planning saves 10 minutes in execution."

~ BRIAN TRACY, TIME-MANAGEMENT EXPERT

Time management is really self-management. We all get the same amount of time each day. What really matters is how we choose to spend that time. And one vitally important key to spending our time more wisely is becoming a pro at prioritizing!

I have yet to meet an assistant that doesn't have a to-do list that's a mile long. No matter how much we get done in a day, the large volume of daily to-dos, files, and electronic communications inevitably pile up and become overwhelming if we aren't good at prioritizing.

To handle all of these tasks and requests, it's important to develop a system that delivers consistent and positive results, and helps you manage the influx. You also need to become a power user of the software programs and tools that can help you organize, manage, and execute your responsibilities.

Hone Your Prioritization Skills

To prioritize means determining the order for handling items or tasks according to their relative importance. You must be able to quickly determine the difference between the important, urgent, and unnecessary. The person standing over your desk with a request may appear urgent, but the customer call you just put on hold may be more important. You also need to realize priorities shift and change throughout the day, sometimes within an hour of when they're set. When your executive is stranded at the airport due to a canceled flight, that becomes the priority over the report you're working on. It's also tempting to choose the three or four smaller tasks on your list that you think you can get done quickly when your time would be better spent doing the one big thing that was of higher value to your company.

In this chapter, we'll look at several ways you can gain insights into how to prioritize more effectively. Daily planning is key in helping you master the skill of prioritizing because it forces you to evaluate what's important, look closely at the timelines and due dates, and assess where you can provide the most value each and every day. Daily meetings with your executive are an opportunity to ask about priorities and gain insight into where you can provide the most value to your company. And creating a master list that contains everything you need to be paying attention to on a daily, weekly, monthly, and annual basis will help because you don't have to worry about forgetting something important.

Let's look at some specific strategies for organizing your time.

Daily Planning Time

Every productivity expert on the planet will tell you that daily planning is crucial. How you choose to tackle your day depends on your work style and environment, but the key is to plan and prioritize daily. No exceptions.

Due to the constant changes that occur throughout the business day, I recommend three planning checkpoints. Allow at least 10 to 15 minutes for planning at the beginning of the day, five to 10 minutes at midday (sometime before or after lunch), and 15 to 20 minutes at the end of the day (before you go home). If this isn't enough, extend the planning time at the end of the day so you're well-prepared for the next day.

If you take 15 minutes at the end of each day to plan, you could potentially save yourself 2.5 hours the following day, according to time-management expert Brian Tracy. If each minute of planning can save you 10 minutes, as Tracy claims, that's a 900% return on your time and energy investment! Plus, it gives you time to think about your plan of attack for the next day before you arrive at the office in the morning.

Keep in mind that, on average, every person has about 90 minutes of high-focus time per day. This is different for each person, and knowing when yours is can help you structure your day so you are working on the most critical items that require the most brain power at your best time of the day. This will help you plan and prioritize your day more successfully.

When you combine this daily planning practice with a daily huddle or planning meeting with your executive, you'll not only stay on top of the priorities, but you'll be able to adjust more quickly when changes occur.

Daily Meetings With Your Executive

Meeting with your executive on a daily basis can make a huge difference in how you organize your time, tasks, and projects. This meeting gives you a chance to get direction on scheduling and project priorities, ask questions, share updates, and provide insights to your executive or manager. It doesn't have to be a long meeting to be effective, but it does need to be a daily habit. The more prepared you are before you meet, the more efficient these meetings will be, and the more willing your executive will be to carve time out of his or her schedule for you.

It's best if you can set aside 15 to 30 minutes at the same time each day even if you don't need the full amount of time, but that's not always possible or practical. If you can't meet face to face with your executive, find a way to talk with them by phone. You need and deserve that one-on-one interaction with your executive if you're expected to stay on top of all of the daily priorities and incoming requests. In time, your executive will also come to value and appreciate these daily planning and debrief sessions if you make each one productive by coming to the meeting or call prepared.

Project Management Tools

Another way to improve your time management is with a project management tool. Many third-party software tools are available. Many email tools incorporate contacts, tasks, calendars, and email so you can use them collectively to manage your time, tasks, and projects. If you're currently using a tool such as Microsoft Outlook or Gmail, I encourage you to become a power user of the software. Learn everything you can about how to use it as a project management tool – beyond just sending and receiving email or managing a random list of tasks.

For example, in Microsoft Outlook, you can use categories and color coding to keep your projects organized and grouped together. Here's how I set up categories to organize my projects and tasks.

Create general categories such as:

- My Team

- Writing

- Speaking

- Client Projects

- Business Development

- Personal

- Research This

If you want your categories list to show up in a particular order, use numbers or symbols in front of each category name. When you alphabetize a list that starts with numbers, the order is obvious. For symbols, it's not as intuitive.

Here is the hierarchy of symbols when placed in alphabetical order with a "file name" or category title following it:

- file name (hyphen)

! file name

file name

$ file name

% file name

& file name

* file name (can't use asterisk in file or folder names, but can be used in Outlook category names)

@ file name

^ file name

_ file name (underscore)

~ file name

+ file name

If I want the categories above to appear in a specific order, adding a symbol from this list to the beginning of each one will help me achieve this. Here is how they will appear when sorted in alphabetical order because of the symbol I've added to the beginning of each category name:

! Speaking

Writing

$ Business Development

$ Client Projects

@ My Team

^ Research This

~ Personal

I use symbols primarily in Outlook Tasks for project management purposes. Some symbols can be used in file names, but not all of them. Keep in mind that numbers work in almost every situation, but symbols that are used in website addresses may not work in file names for all programs (e.g. #, &, ?, etc.)

You may have a lot more task or project categories than this, so these are just ideas to get you started. In Outlook, you can also assign a color to each category. These categories can then be assigned to tasks, calendar appointments, and emails to add continuity and organization across all Outlook components. I will share more about project management in a later chapter.

 Resource Alert: There are also many online, third-party tools and project management platforms designed to integrate with your current email program by installing a plugin or application. Visit **TheOrganizedAdmin.com** to find some options. Then do some research to determine which one will work best for your specific needs.

Master Lists, Daily Lists, and Prioritizing

When it comes to making lists, I'm a pen-and-paper person. I can organize my thoughts and prioritize better when I do it on paper. And there's a good reason why. It's been scientifically shown that when you write things down, connections occur between your head and hand that do not occur when you type. Writing strengthens the learning process. Our brain receives feedback from our motor actions, together with the sensation of touching a pen and paper.[13] Writing can help you think more clearly about the important things you need to do and the best plan of attack for doing them.

Yet, creating lists by hand can be unorganized and unwieldy…if you don't have a good system in place for prioritizing them and taking action. If you find yourself working from a pile of sticky notes and notepads all day, it's time to rethink your to-do list strategy!

When it comes to capturing, tracking, and completing tasks, you must have a system that you follow religiously. Where do you record new tasks? Where do you enter them so they can be tracked and referred to until they are checked off and completed? In this digital age, your system will most likely integrate paper and digital to keep you on track.

If you prefer to use paper for your lists, I recommend writing your thoughts down first. Then type them into Outlook Tasks or a project management tool so you can keep track of them digitally. Having a digital record will also make it very easy to sort lists by priority, project categories, dates, or keywords. However, if it's helpful, you can still create a short list on paper each day that includes your top priorities or tasks, and then check them off as they're completed.

Another option is to make a master project list in a word processing document or spreadsheet and create your daily to-do list from this master file. If you choose this method, be sure to include key fields such as project type, start date, due date, and priority level so it's easy to sort and review on a daily basis.

When you implement daily planning into your schedule, you review the tasks you accomplished at the end of each day and roll the outstanding to-do list items to the next day or reprioritize them based on importance or urgency. Then you review what's coming up for the next day on your master list, and prioritize the tasks according to your peak energy levels, availability, and the other tasks and projects on your list. Keep in mind, it's probably not practical or realistic to have 20 items on your to-do list for tomorrow. Narrow your list down to your top seven or 10 items. If you get them all done, you can always revisit your master list and add a couple more. It will help you reduce overwhelm and get the most important things accomplished each day.

Paper, electronic, short, or long – it really doesn't matter what list making method you choose! What's important is that you have a system for capturing and organizing your tasks and ideas so you can follow through and execute them effectively every single day.

Managing Recurring Tasks

Once you have a good task management system in place, managing recurring tasks becomes easier, too. Many recurring tasks can be automated with Outlook Tasks, or your project management tool, and a good tickler file system that provides weekly or monthly reminders.

There are many ways you can set up a paper-based tickler file system (see chapter 8), including:

- **Weekly:** Monday through Friday files

- **Monthly:** January through December files

- **Monthly and Daily:** January through December files with 1 to 31 files behind them for each day of the month. (These daily files rotate from month to month, so you only have one set of 1 to 31.)

If you prefer to go the digital route, you can set up electronic ticklers with your project management tool or recurring tasks within your email tool. Most tools offer the ability to sync ticklers with your electronic calendars, so you get daily, weekly, or monthly task reminders.

Even though the dream of a paperless office floats around, most offices still need a hybrid system of electronic and paper tickler files. Your digital reminders appear on the dates you set, and the coordinating file folder in your tickler system contains the details and paperwork related to completing the task.

Like list-making, your tickler systems should fit your personal preferences. It really doesn't matter what method you choose – as long as you have a solid reminder system in place and you use it consistently.

Scheduling Time for Tasks and Projects

Most admins are great at keeping track of all of their tasks and to-dos. Where they fall short is in planning for or scheduling enough time to complete the tasks and projects on their lists, especially with the constant interruptions and unplanned projects.

If you're working on a new task or project, it may take a little trial and error the first time or two. Eventually, you'll get a better grasp of it and how long it takes to complete, which will make scheduling it easier. The challenge for a lot of assistants is factoring in the nonstop interruptions and distractions.

One way to troubleshoot this is by keeping a time log for a week or two. How long does it really take you to do that report – even with the disruptions factored in? How many phone calls do you take in a day? How much time are you spending on email management? How much project time do you have in the average workday? All of this is vital data when planning or having discussions with your executive about how to improve processes for better time management. Keeping a time log helps you develop a stronger time awareness. Before you start your log, you may want to estimate how long you think various tasks will take. Then record how long it actually took. Knowing the time difference between the two can help you adjust how you schedule your time to accomplish the tasks going forward.

Once you have a time log, do some analysis so you can attach a specific amount of time to your daily tasks. Let's say you're typically at the office from 8 a.m. to 5 p.m. That's nine hours of time each workday. If you take a lunch break, that probably consumes 30 to 60 minutes. Your beginning-of-the-day procedures for getting your computer turned on, voicemail checked, doors and files unlocked, etc., probably consumes at least 15 to 20 minutes. The same applies to your end-of-the-day shutting-down procedures. Hopefully you allow at least 15 to 30 minutes of planning time each day. This means you're already down to about seven hours remaining. How much time do you spend on email management, answering phone calls, and handling the general day-to-day job responsibilities? How much time do you spend socializing with co-workers? Your time log will help you track this. Let's say your daily responsibilities take around four hours each day. That only leaves you with three hours for specific tasks or projects on your list. If we're realistic, we know a certain percentage of our day is consumed by unexpected requests or other "emergencies," so we should also reserve some time for those.

With firm numbers in mind, you can use this information during your daily planning sessions to schedule or reserve the right amount of time for tasks and projects on your priority list. You'll still have to remain flexible and allow for changes. But this process gives you a more accurate picture of what your day looks like, which will help you be more successful in making it happen.

File Download: Need help creating your time log? Get your template at **TheOrganizedAdmin.com.**

Use Checklists for Everything

As admins, we pride ourselves in being able to remember all of the details. But the more information that comes at us, the harder it is to remember everything. This is why I use checklists for just about everything.

I have checklists for travel planning, meeting planning, and setting up teleconferences. I have daily startup and shutdown checklists so I don't forget to do basic things or get distracted on my way in or out. I even use checklists to ensure I take daily action on my professional goals. They are easy to create and keep me on track so I don't forget or neglect important details.

Here is an example of a checklist I created to keep me on track during the day:

Beginning of the day:

- ☐ Unlock doors.

- ☐ Turn off forwarding on phones.

- ☐ Check voice messages.

- ☐ Log into PC.

- ☐ Read emails.

- ☐ Check/review calendars for today: (executive's name).

- ☐ Check tickler files.

- ☐ Pick up notes/mail from weekend.

- ☐ Review in-tray Items that came over the weekend.

- ☐ Turn copier on.

☐ Turn lamp/light on.

☐ Meet with (executive's/manager's name) to review priorities for the day.

During the day:

☐ Phones

☐ Mail

☐ Visitors

☐ Projects

End of the day:

☐ 3 p.m. – Check with (executive's/manager's name) to see what else we need to get done before the end of the day.

☐ Review tomorrow's projects/tasks.

☐ Review calendars for next day: (executive's name).

☐ Clear inbox tray.

☐ 4:30 p.m. – Print (executive's name)'s daily calendar page for the next day. (On Friday, also print a week-at-a-glance page for the next week.)

☐ Clear desktop.

☐ Lock file drawers.

☐ Make sure the coffee pot is turned off.

- ☐ 5 p.m. – Forward phone, log out of computer, turn copier off.

- ☐ Turn lamp/light off.

- ☐ Lock front door.

Weekly items:

- ☐ Water plants (lobby, executive's office).

- ☐ Email kitchen cleaning schedule reminders and follow-up.

- ☐ Perform office supply ordering/purchasing.

- ☐ Stock water in the fridge for executive's guests.

- ☐ Create weekly team in/out schedule and post on bulletin board.

Monthly items:

- ☐ Email cleaning/dusting schedule reminders and follow-up.

- ☐ Recycle office paper.

I used to keep this checklist on a bulletin board next to my computer monitor so I could quickly reference it to ensure I'd done the basics each day. Not having to remember all of these things allowed me to better focus on the day's priorities and not worry about forgetting something.

While my list likely won't match your tasks and schedule, I strongly encourage you to use this as a starting point to create your own. It can be a lifesaver on days when you're really busy or something unexpected pops up!

There are only so many hours in each day to accomplish what we need to get done. While you can't create extra time, you can save yourself a good chunk of it by using to-do lists and tasks along with project and calendar management tools to make yourself more efficient! Test them out and create a system that works best for you.

PLAN OF ACTION:

☐ Do you have a set time each day for daily planning? If not, start by spending 30 minutes before you leave the office each day to wrap things up and map out your plan of action for tomorrow. Repeat this daily.

☐ When you get to the office in the morning, review your plan of action again and make any necessary adjustments based on information or messages that have come in overnight.

☐ Do you have a daily meeting with your executive? If not, it's time to initiate this daily best practice. It may take a little time and convincing if it's not something your executive has ever done before, but it's worth it!

☐ Identify what your system is for recording, tracking, and completing your tasks and projects. Is it paper? Digital? A hybrid of both? Write it out on paper so you can see it and think through it logically.

☐ Do you know how much time you truly have to work on important tasks and projects each day? If not, keep a time log for at least five days to give yourself some insights into how long things take and where you're spending your time.

☐ What are some helpful checklists you can create to help you stay on track and remember all the details without overloading your brain? Create one today. Add it to your procedures binder. Then create your next checklist tomorrow. Repeat.

Part 3: Organizing Work and Projects

If only getting organized were as easy as organizing our ideas, workspace, and time! Now let's apply the basic principles of organization to some of the more complex work and projects you deal with every day:

- Inbox Organization

- Meeting and Event Organization

- Travel Planning Organization Project Organization

Chapter 10

Inbox Organization

"Self-management enables email management."
~ MARSHA EGAN, AUTHOR OF *INBOX DETOX*

I have a confession to make: Email is my biggest organization challenge.

My inbox used to be under control and manageable when I worked corporately and supported multiple executives. I used to think it was ridiculous that several of my executives had inboxes with hundreds – even thousands – of emails in them.

Then I became a business owner and my own inbox exploded. At one point, I was managing up to 10 email accounts for various client projects. I was still using Microsoft Outlook, so the software functionality was the same. However, my email volume increased exponentially when I started my virtual assistant business, and my inbox was suddenly overflowing.

I would get my inbox under control for short periods, but I couldn't keep it in check. So I started looking for books, training, and experts to help me. Many experts had similar best practices for email management. Some of their tips would help for a while, but then I'd sink right back into my same old bad habits. I was frustrated by my own lack of discipline.

My breakthrough came when I heard Laura Stack, a productivity expert and Microsoft Outlook trainer, explain that Outlook has several features to help users optimally leverage the email program. However, these settings aren't part of the software's default settings, which means most people aren't using Outlook efficiently or to its fullest potential.

Empowered by this knowledge, I decided to hit reset on my strategy for email management. I started searching for Outlook training options. I encourage admins to become power users of the software tools they use, so I took my own advice.

Part of the challenge with my inbox was creating good habits and applying discipline to the process. When I'm disciplined about my inbox management daily, I am successful in keeping my email processed out of my inbox. When I lose focus, or don't allow enough time to recover after a busy project period or upon my return from being out of the office, I struggle to get caught back up.

When a change in personal behavior is required, there's no quick fix, unfortunately. So, I enlisted the support of a productivity and organization coach to hold me accountable and help me efficiently navigate the process. The result was a clean inbox for processing mail (not storing it), the knowledge on how to use Outlook to its fullest potential, and these best practices.

Use Folders for Sorting, Not Storing

Think of folders as an inbox sorting mechanism, not a storage location. Many companies have inbox limitations that require judiciousness with email folder storage. Even if you can get exceptions to the storage cap, it's more efficient to save important emails to a shared network folder with your other project files. Outlook has a file extension called .msg just like Word has .doc or Excel has .xls. When you save (or copy/paste) an Outlook email message to your shared network folders, you can then open it just like you would any other file.

Taking this approach to saving important emails will keep you organized because now all of your digital files will be in the same location on your shared network drive instead of in your email and on the network.

Automate With Rules

Rules allow you to automate the sorting and prioritizing process of going through your inbox. They are created for sending general correspondence – such as sale flyers, advertisements, or newsletters – to a specific folder. By removing the item from your inbox, you won't spend more time on it than it deserves. This doesn't mean you never look at it; this simply means you choose when you look at it because it's not urgent or important.

Create Tasks

Any inbox item that requires action needs to be moved to a task. Your tasks then become a master to-do list and daily action item lists that you can prioritize and keep visible. When you move an email to a task in Microsoft Outlook, the original email remains intact and attached to the task so you can reply to the original email at any point.

It's important to note that when you drag (instead of move) an email into the Outlook Tasks folder, the original email is copied into the body of the task, but the original message is not included as an attachment. So moving an item to your Tasks folder is better than dragging it if you want to be able to reply to the original message upon completion of the task.

This best practice gets you out of your inbox and into working from a prioritized task list. It also helps you focus your time and attention on the day's priorities and minimizes distractions from new emails.

Calendar Appointments

An inbox item that requires you to be somewhere at a specific date and time should be moved to your calendar. When you move an email to your calendar, it will also remain intact and attached to your calendar appointment. If you receive a calendar invite from someone, simply click Accept and it will automatically be added to your calendar. For invitations that come in message format, you can easily convert them to an appointment by using the Move feature in Outlook.

How to Start Fresh With Your Inbox

In addition to using these basic Outlook principles as the foundation for your email management system, I also recommend that you create an archive folder called OLD INBOX. Then move all your emails out of your inbox and into that folder so you can start with a clean inbox. This will help you feel less overwhelmed and allow you to get a better handle on your new approach.

Once you have a clean inbox, click on your old email archive folder. You can sort your emails by name to do some quick cleanup of old newsletters, ads, and general notifications that aren't important. Trust me, it will feel good to delete entire blocks of email!

Next, sort your archived emails by date and scan through the list to determine if there are important ones you need to handle. When you find one, convert it to a task or calendar appointment. I suggest going back about 30 days on your initial review. If you have time, you can go back and search a bit further back. It's probably not practical or worth your time to go through every single email in the archive folder once you pull the important things from it. Plus, you can always refer back to it if needed.

Finally, you need to focus on the new emails arriving in your inbox. It's vital that you empty your inbox every single day. This doesn't mean that you answered every single message; it simply means you processed it and placed it in the appropriate place (task list, calendar, folder, reference file, or trash). Once you do this, it's ready for what needs to happen to it next. If you can quickly do it on the spot, do it. If you can't, process it to the appropriate location.

As new emails start to pour in, try to avoid letting junk clutter up your inbox. Unsubscribe from emails that aren't relevant. Create rules to filter newsletters and promotional emails that you want to read when you have time. These things don't need to take up valuable space in your inbox. You may also want to turn off social media notifications if you're not responsible for managing work-related accounts. These notices not only clog up your inbox, but they can be really distracting.

 Resource Alert: Find additional email organization and productivity resources at **TheOrganizedAdmin.com**.

This new approach to email management will probably take a few days — maybe even a week or two — to get used to. But once you clear out the old stuff, create rules, and get rid of the junk, you and your inbox will be in much better shape. You may even start to see some wonderful productivity side effects!

On occasion, you will fall behind on keeping up with your inbox. It can feel so defeating. When this happens, pay attention to what just created the situation. Were you head-down on a big project for a few days and now your inbox is overflowing again? Did you just return from being out of the office for a few days? By pinpointing the specifics of what created the situation, you can be more proactive in planning for them in the future. For me, I need to schedule time on my calendar following a trip or vacation to process email. It's not something I can simply work into my normal day. It requires a dedicated time period to get back on top of things again. Now, I'm getting better at scheduling blocks of time for email recovery when I return from time out of the office. I encourage you to do the same.

When I began working from my task list instead of my inbox, my entire approach to getting things done shifted. I felt more in control of my day. I felt more in control of my time. I knew exactly what I needed to do next when I finished up one thing and was ready to move onto the next. It was a very liberating feeling. It didn't mean that my to-do list was shorter. It meant that I wasn't scrolling back through hundreds of emails looking for things, or wondering if I'd overlooked something important. The relief I felt was incredible. I hope that by taking this new approach to email management, you will feel the same way!

PLAN OF ACTION:

☐ Create an email folder called: OLD INBOX – [today's date]

☐ Move all emails from your inbox to this OLD INBOX folder.

☐ As new emails come into your inbox, take action in one of these ways:

    ☐ Do it...if you can do it quickly (in three minutes or less) and get it off your list.

    ☐ Create a rule and/or folder to automatically filter it.

    ☐ Create a task (if it's something you need to do).

    ☐ Create a calendar appointment (if it's somewhere you need to be).

    ☐ Save it to your hard drive (if you need it for reference).

    ☐ Delete it.

☐ Process your email in batches, and go through every single email each day. Practice making a decision about what to do with each message.

☐ Work from your task list each day, not from your inbox.

☐ Create a special alert rule for emails from your executive to ensure you are immediately notified of incoming messages from them. This will help you get comfortable with working from your task list instead of your inbox!

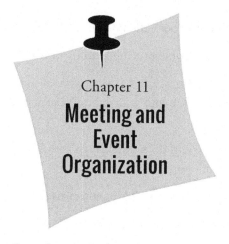

Chapter 11

Meeting and Event Organization

"Success depends upon previous preparation, and without such preparation there is sure to be failure."
~ CONFUCIUS

Up to this chapter, I've talked about organizing the various components of your overall work systems. Now I'm going to look at organizing projects and workload. As an admin, organization is a vital part of everything you do, but one place where it's absolutely crucial is in planning and executing meetings and events.

How do you stay on top of all the moving parts of organizing meetings and events? How do you apply the organizing principles you've learned to projects?

One of my favorite ways is by creating thorough checklists, forms, and templates. Let's apply the basic organizing principles to this process:

1. **Gather similar items together.** Do a brain dump of all the planning elements that go into each type of meeting or event that you plan. You may need a separate list for each event if you have a diverse range of meeting types you're responsible for. Or you may be able to do one master list with specific subsections for specific meeting types, such as staff meetings, board meetings, client meetings, etc.

2. **Contain the items.** Once you have all of your planning elements outlined on paper, put them in a formal document and order them chronologically by how you typically handle them.

3. **Label the items.** Name your checklist or planning form in a way that you will be able to easily find it again or search for it on your computer with keywords (e.g., "FORM – Meeting and Event Planning" or "CHECKLIST – Meeting and Event Planning").

4. **Create a home for the items.** If you don't already have a Forms & Templates folder on your computer, create one. Then save your forms, templates, and checklists to this folder so you can always find them quickly.

Once your digital copy is created and saved, create a paper file folder with the same title as your digital file and place it within arm's reach of where you sit during the day. Or place it in your administrative procedures binder. The goal is for these forms to be easy to retrieve when your executive starts rattling off details for a meeting or event that you need to set up.

Having these planning forms at your fingertips will allow you to quickly capture more details from your executive because you'll have the visual triggers on the page in front of you. Your executive may not have the answers to every question initially, but forms help you get more information faster, and they make you and your executive more efficient in getting meetings and events set up.

Become an Event COP!

Now that you understand the overall approach, the next step is to look at the details and smaller parts involved in event planning. There's a lot that goes into a successful event. If you want to stay organized and impress your colleagues, you need to become an event COP: creative, organized, project manager!

Becoming an event COP requires breaking down the main components of event planning and learning best practices to apply to each. To do that, you need to apply creativity, organization, and project management to the planning, implementation, and management of your meetings and events.

Unleash Your Creative Side

When you think about the details of event planning, you probably think of checklists, calling vendors, coordinating calendars, and a seemingly endless list of tasks. What many admins overlook about event planning is the creativity that goes into putting together a successful and enjoyable event.

There are a variety of ways to get creative when coordinating a meeting or event, and doing so can help your event be more enjoyable and memorable. Even small things – such as a theme, giveaways, or snacks – can make a big difference.

With information as plentiful as it is today, it's easy to find resources dedicated to event planning that can help you come up with unique elements for your event. Browse through magazines and websites. Take pictures of good ideas you find while shopping or attending events yourself. Inspiration is everywhere. Use a OneNote notebook or Pinterest boards to capture ideas so you have a catalog to refer to later.

Using the wisdom of others in the industry is a great way to expand your knowledge and find new techniques, ideas, and best practices to try at your event. Start compiling your own list of publications and websites that inspire your inner event planner so you have a reference anytime you need it!

Impress Your Guests Without Busting Your Budget

Adding extras to an event can seem daunting and financially draining, especially on top of everything else that goes into a corporate event. But incentives don't have to be difficult or expensive. There are plenty of free or inexpensive ways to add pizzazz to your event. Even small things can leave a big impression on guests, so give some of these budget-friendly ideas a try at your next event:

- A theme

- Team-building activities, like a scavenger hunt, puzzle, or trivia game

- Table treats, such as bottles of water, notepads, or candy

- Attendee gifts, such as hats or T-shirts

- Blotters and/or agenda cards

- Pens or highlighters

- Company promotional items

- Event guides

- Centerpieces (like flowers, signs, or candles)

- Food and beverages

- Attendance incentives, such as continuing education credit or certificates

- Early-arrival incentives, like a pre-event breakfast or a goody bag

- Colored/labeled folders

- Name tents

- Chair massages

Make sure to consider the nature of your event and who your guests will be before deciding on your incentives or give-aways. Trivia games and ice cream sundaes might work well for a company retreat, but they're not really appropriate for most board meetings. As you try different ideas on this list, or ones you find on your own, you'll start to learn what works well for you and what generates the best responses from guests. Also, as you try new ideas and gain more experience, keep your own list of fun, budget-friendly ideas so you have a reference for upcoming events.

Leverage Your Event Organization

If your meeting or event isn't organized and executed efficiently and competently, any creative touches won't matter. So staying on top of organization when planning and executing an event is a top priority. This requires breaking down, organizing, and managing all aspects of your event or meeting.

1. **Develop forms and templates to simplify the event planning process.** As I mentioned earlier, having templates to help you with meeting or event preparation not only helps you be more organized, but it's also a huge timesaver. Meeting agendas, client checklists, and event itineraries are just a few examples of the types of templates you should have created and ready to use. To give you a better idea of the kinds of forms and templates you should consider, here are a few of the ones I've created and used over the years:

- Board Meeting Agenda
- Board Meeting Planning Form
- Board Meeting Invitation (email template)
- Conference Agenda
- Conference Planning Project Plan
- Conference Timeline Day of Event
- Meeting Agenda for Client Site Visits
- Meeting Planning Form – Executive Team
- Meeting Planning Form – GENERAL
- Meeting Planning Form – Staff Meetings
- Name Tents
- Trade Show Details Event Schedule
- Trade Show Event Research

- Travel Arrangements Checklist

- Travel Itinerary

- Travel Profile

2. **Identify key suppliers and cultivate relationships.** Reliable vendors and suppliers are the foundation of any event. Identifying key suppliers and vendors, and forming relationships with them, helps ensure that you have the people and services you need to put together a great event.

   Finding the best vendors and suppliers can take a little trial and error. The best thing you can do if you're new to event planning is ask for recommendations from others in your company or throughout your professional network who've worked with vendors in your area. Have you attended an event that was particularly well put together or impressively catered? Reach out to the event coordinator and find out the names of their suppliers.

   Once you have your go-to vendors, keep a detailed list of them. This list should include their contact information, services they provide, prices, and the types of events to use them for.

   Here are a few of the basic suppliers and vendors you should have on your list:

   - **Venues**

     ◦ Hotels

     ◦ Event Centers

     ◦ Meeting Rooms (at your company)

- **Travel Partners**
  - Ground Transportation
  - Airlines
  - Buses / Minibuses
- **Food and Beverage Suppliers**
- **Event Services and Rental Companies**
- **Technical Production** (e.g., audio/visual, lighting, sound)
- **Media Production** (e.g., photography, videography)
- **Collateral Materials** (e.g., signage, printed materials, promotional items)

3. **Review your company policies.** The last thing you want to find out mid-event is that something you planned and paid for violates company policy. So review all company policies before moving forward with planning for any event, office party, or large meeting. Checking company policy is a detail that's easy to overlook when it comes to putting something like this together, but a small slip-up could ruin an entire event.

Some company policies to review include:

- Alcohol policy
- Budget and expense report policy
- Corporate incentives for hosting a green or eco-friendly event

- Distribution of confidential documents in print or digitally

Once you do your research, keep copies of any relevant company policies with the rest of your event planning materials. Don't stop at just company policies either. If you're planning an event at a venue, you'll need to review its policies and communicate them to your event planners and attendees appropriately too.

Develop the Project Manager Within

Event planning is project management. It is a multi-faceted job that requires meticulous attention to detail, organization, and a lot of patience. A big part of successful event planning is being able to anticipate the needs of your guests and the expectations of your executive while effectively managing the project.

Detailed and organized lists can help you keep track of the upcoming tasks, possible venues, alternate plans, and other important aspects of your meeting or event. Use these lists to keep tabs on exactly what you're doing and what needs done during the planning and management of your meeting or event.

Compile a list of the types of meetings and events your company holds. From there, you can branch out into specific tasks, vendors, and travel plans associated with each type of event. This list of basic meeting and event types will get you started, but make sure to add any additional ones that are specific to your company.

Types of Meetings:

- Annual appreciation events

- Board of directors meetings

- Client meetings (on site and off site)

- Company social events, such as holiday parties or picnics

- Conferences

- Golf tournaments

- Monthly executive meetings

- Multiday events with external guests

- One-on-one meetings

- Project status meetings

- Sales- or incentive-based awards trips

- Seminars

- Service awards banquets

- Strategic retreats

- Tours

- Training sessions

- Weekly staff meetings

What I Use: To see my sample event planning form, visit **TheOrganizedAdmin.com**.

Have a Backup Plan

When planning any meeting or event, you must think about contingency options in case things don't go according to your plans. You have to anticipate possible problems and have a corresponding backup plan for each scenario. For example, if you're planning an outdoor event, have a plan in case of bad weather. If you have a speaker flying in, you need a plan for delayed or canceled flights.

Here are some meeting details you need to have backup plans for:

- Meeting space or venue

- Speakers and/or meeting leaders

- IT and media services

- Handouts, materials, and agendas

- Reservations and RSVPs (too many, too few, or no responses at all)

- Budget

- Food and catering

- Facilities and maintenance requests

- Working with volunteers, committees, staff, etc.

- Signage

I was part of an event planning team that had a speaker fail to show because the speaker didn't have us listed on her calendar correctly. These things happen. In the moment, we brainstormed with the speakers we already had onsite at the event to create an alternative option for the missing speaker's segment. Following that event, we updated our checklists to include a verbal confirmation by phone with our speaker a month, a week, and the day before the event.

When your event is finished, I strongly encourage you to hold a post-event meeting or review to analyze what went well, what could have gone better, and what you'd change if you did it again. Take detailed notes. Update your planning checklists and forms. Use the insights you've gained in managing this event planning project to your future events. That's the best way to continually improve your events and impress your colleagues at the same time.

Stay on Top of the Event Planning Industry

We've talked about how to apply organization principles to planning your meetings, and the ins and outs of becoming an event COP. But there's one more simple yet effective strategy for becoming an expert event planner: Stay on top of the event planning industry. Regularly review new resources, vendors, and best practices that can help you continuously sharpen your event planning, managing, and organizing skills.

Here are a few ways to keep tabs on what's going on in the event planning world:

- Read magazines and industry publications.

- Read websites and blogs.

- Subscribe to e-newsletters.

- Join professional associations specific to event planning.

- Get certified as a meeting planning professional.

- Attend events and conferences for event planning.

- Talk to other event and meeting planners.

- Join relevant LinkedIn groups.

- "Like" relevant Facebook pages.

- Search for ideas on social media sites such as Pinterest.

A lot goes into planning an event or meeting. Without proper organization and smooth execution, you run the risk of disappointing your guests, team, and executive. Keep everyone happy and yourself less stressed by putting the best practices, lists, and other resources from this chapter to use the next time you have an event to plan!

Just remember: You only have so much control over what happens at an event. But if you're organized and think like an event planner, even the occasional hiccup won't prevent you from hosting a great event.

PLAN OF ACTION:

☐ Make a list of the typical meetings and events you coordinate.

☐ Do you have planning checklists, forms, or templates for any of the items on your list?

    ☐ If yes, pull them together in one location digitally and/or in print.

    ☐ If no, then begin creating these.

☐ Create a section in your procedures binder or a paper folder for storing extra copies of these forms so they are easily accessible when you need them.

☐ Create a desktop shortcut on your computer so you can quickly navigate to the digital file location of these forms, templates, and checklists.

☐ Create an Events folder on your computer and subfolders for the types of events you coordinate (e.g., board meetings, staff meetings, client site visits). Create a subfolder in each of these folders with the date of the event you are planning. Then save the planning details for each event in its respective folder so you (or anyone helping you) can always find what you need.

 What I Use: To see a sample folder structure from my file directory, visit **TheOrganizedAdmin.com**.

☐ Identify at least one new way to find new ideas and stay current on event and meeting planning best practices.

Chapter 12
Travel Planning Organization

"Most travel is best of all in the anticipation or the remembering; the reality has more to do with losing your luggage."
~ REGINA NADELSON, NOVELIST

Coordinating travel for your executives – or anyone other than yourself – can be challenging whether you're brand new to travel planning or a seasoned pro. From coordinating the countless details to handling spur-of-the-moment emergencies, such as delayed or canceled flights, travel planning is an ongoing responsibility. But there are a lot of things you can do to make organizing travel plans less stressful, more enjoyable, and even downright fun.

Develop a Travel Planner's Mindset
The challenge with organizing travel planning is there are so many moving parts and last-minute changes that can throw the most

beautifully organized trip into a tailspin. The issues that come up may not be your fault, but you still have to work through them to get your traveler where he or she needs to be on time.

If you want to be prepared for the adventure that is corporate travel planning, you must start by developing a travel planner's mindset. Here are a few key things that will help you maintain a more balanced perspective as a travel planner.

1. Accept that nothing is ever set in stone. Every element of any trip is always subject to change.

2. When you start planning a trip, think about contingency plans and how you can proactively prepare for things that may come up while your executive is traveling.

3. Remain calm when you encounter a problem, such as a flight delay, canceled flight, or frustrated executive. You need to think clearly to resolve things quickly.

4. Educate yourself on the tools and resources that can help you successfully accomplish your travel planning duties.

5. Be willing to ask for help, and know when you need it. For example, if you're planning an international trip or complex itinerary, you may need assistance from a travel agent.

6. Travel planning isn't about you — it's about your traveler. Make sure you fully understand their expectations, wants, and needs.

7. Remember, travel planning is 100% service-based and customer-focused. Ask yourself, "How can I provide not just a service, but a value-added service to the travelers I support?"

Travel has become a lot more complex than it used to be. It's stressful trying to get through security, airlines now charge fees at every turn, and there are fewer flight options. Keep all of this in mind as you send your traveler out the door.

Anything you can do to counter-balance these travel stresses – including providing calm, reassuring support and sharing the value-added components (which we'll talk more about throughout this chapter) – can help ease your traveler's mind and make you look like a travel planning superstar!

Best Practices to Systematize Travel Planning

Once you have the right travel planning mindset, you need to adopt some best practices to systematize the process as much as possible.

Best Practice #1: Develop a relationship with a local travel agency that's affiliated with a national brand.

Professional, experienced travel agents can be a huge help when it comes to travel planning. They have extensive knowledge of the travel industry and frequently can access tickets, suppliers, and prices that are unavailable to the masses.

If you don't work for a company that has an in-house travel department, it's important to establish a relationship with a travel agency. (Check with your human resources department to see if your company has a preferred provider before you seek out a new one.) This helps to ensure you have a trusted, reliable adviser who you can turn to if and when you need travel assistance. It also gives you access to their online booking tools, which typically save time and money.

An agency usually charges a ticketing fee, but so do other online tools. (You may not see it, but they do!) I've always thought of the agency ticketing fee as my own personal travel insurance because I know I have experts who can help me if anything goes wrong while my executive is traveling.

Throughout the years, my travel agents have saved me thousands of dollars. They've corrected mistakes I've made – like booking a first-class plane ticket to Hawaii on the wrong date. They've secured better seats at better prices than I found online. And they've helped me quickly get stranded travelers back on their path when something went haywire.

Having a travel agency doesn't mean you have to call them every time you need to book a trip. Many agencies have online booking tools that you can use to make reservations on your own. However, you may want to consider employing their assistance for the following:

- First-class airline tickets

- Refundable airline tickets

- International travel

- Multi-stop trips

- Any trip that requires research to figure out the best options at the executive's destination. (I once timed my travel research, and it took me two hours to do what my travel agent did in less than 20 minutes!)

Best Practice #2: Know your company's travel policies.
If your company has an established corporate travel policy, make sure you know and understand it. Which colleagues can fly first

class? Can top-level executives fly on the same flights, or do they have to fly separately? What is the daily food allowance? What is the mileage reimbursement policy? Being aware of these things will help you educate your traveler and keep you out of trouble, too.

Best Practice #3: Know your company's preferred suppliers.

If your company has agreements with national brands for car services, rental cars, airfares, or hotels, you need to know which companies to use and their rates. Even if a cheaper travel rate is available, you may still need to make your reservations through your company's preferred supplier due to additional benefits or group purchasing power.

Best Practice #4: Develop standard travel forms, templates, and checklists.

Forms, templates, and checklists are big lifesavers – so much so that I devoted a whole chapter of this book to them! But they are especially useful when coordinating travel for multiple people or multiple trips for the same traveler. There are a lot of details to track. You have to remember what information you need from your traveler. He or she needs to remember to give it to you. It can be a huge headache to keep tabs on it all on your own.

After missing a few important details while planning trips, I wanted to relieve the stress associated with trying to remember all of this information. So I developed several travel planning forms, templates, and checklists that have been instrumental in helping me keep track of everything and everyone.

Travel Planning Forms, Templates, and Checklists

The basic forms, templates, and checklists I use to organize travel planning for my travelers and myself are resources that I've been using since early in my career.

Some of these forms, templates, and checklists are pretty comprehensive, but you may still need to customize them to each traveler's specific needs. Feel free to tweak these for your own use – remove questions and fields you don't need, and add things that are missing. Think of these resources as guides to get you started on creating your own.

The following is a list of the forms, templates, and checklists I use for travel planning, why the information is important, and a few pointers on incorporating them into your travel planning routine.

Travel Profile Form

The travel profile form is designed to capture all of the important data about your executive's travel preferences, frequent flier numbers, company details, and more. It specifically includes:

- Contact details for your travel agency or corporate travel team

- Vital information about your traveler, including their full name, address, cell, home, and office phone numbers, email and home addresses, etc.

- Emergency contact information

- Company cost center/accounting information (for submitting expense reports)

- Frequent flier numbers and statuses

- Seating preferences

- Meal requests

- Car rental preferences

- Hotel preferences

- Passport information

Travel Planning Form

The travel planning form covers all the primary details that need to be reviewed and handled for a traveling executive, including flights (private and commercial), ground transportation, hotel reservations, meal reservations, meeting planning details, and entertainment. Your form should have a section for each specific type of travel planning you need to coordinate for each trip (e.g., one section for flights, one for hotels). This form can be customized to fit your executive's typical travel and meeting planning needs.

 What I Use: To see a sample of my travel planning form, visit **TheOrganizedAdmin.com**.

At the top of each form, include the name of the traveling executive, the type of event they are traveling for (e.g., board meeting, conference, trade show), the location of the meeting (city and state), and the dates of their departure and return.

EXECUTIVE NAME: _____

❑ AIR _____	❑ DINING _____	
❑ CAR _____	❑ MEETINGS ___	
❑ HOTEL ___	❑ ITINERARY ___	

MTG TYPE: _____

LOCATION: _____

DATE(S): _____

Include a checklist at the top left corner of page one to give yourself an overview of what you have completed, and what still needs to be done just by looking at the top cover sheet. Once you complete an element, check the box and put the date next to it so you know at a glance that it's finished.

I typically copy these forms on double-sided colored paper so the colored sheets stand out in my files. Keep this form attached to the top of the packet of travel details as you make the arrangements. You may even want to color-code the travel sheets for each executive with a different color if you plan travel for multiple executives (e.g., executive A on yellow paper, executive B on green paper). Keep multiple blank copies of the form in a folder on your desk for quick and easy access in case your executive starts sharing meeting planning and travel details with you unexpectedly.

Here are a few additional tips to help you in this planning stage:

- Always confirm the *state or country* of the city your traveler is going to. There are a lot of states and countries with the same city names.

- Research restaurants and activities in the area so you can suggest options to your traveler.

- Prepare driving directions/maps for all to/from points on the itinerary, even if your traveler has a GPS.

Travel Itinerary

After all travel plans are arranged and finalized, the last detail is assembling the information into a formal travel itinerary for your executive.

As an administrative professional, it's your responsibility to keep your executive organized and on track – both in the office and while traveling. A travel itinerary is a valuable roadmap for you and your executive that explains exactly where they will be going, what they will be doing, and when. It helps ease the stress of putting a trip together and sending your executive off on the road.

Itineraries save travelers a lot of time and the hassle of sorting through multiple documents or emails to find the information they need. A lot of what they need to know (flights, ground transportation, hotel) may be listed on the travel itinerary that comes from your travel agency. However, it doesn't include details about meetings or entertainment, or extra notes that your customized travel itinerary will.

Creating a travel itinerary is also a great final check of all of the travel information in a logical, chronological view that helps ensure you've completed all of the travel details required for the trip. I've done a lot of traveling, and trips with an itinerary are much more efficient. It helps ensure you and your executive are on the same page for the duration of the trip, and that the trip is as productive and smooth as possible. Don't underestimate the power of putting an itinerary together for all of your executive's travel – you won't regret sweating the details when your exec's trip is a success!

 File Download: If you support traveling teams and executives, download this travel itinerary template to keep yourself organized at **TheOrganizedAdmin.com.**

Coordinating International Travel

Even if you're comfortable making domestic travel arrangements, a lot of admins get nervous planning a trip abroad. But you really don't need to be worried. Organizing an international trip is very similar to a domestic one with three main exceptions: time zone changes, additional travel documents, and foreign currency.

I've done my share of international travel, so I can tell you from personal experience that I prepare for an international trip just like I do a domestic trip. The only major difference is that I need a passport (and possibly a visa), instead of my driver's license. I also pack a travel converter for my electronic devices, and some foreign currency – even if I'm using my credit card. And I always use my travel agency for booking international trips. No exceptions. They can advise and prepare you for your trip in countless ways.

Your checklist for preparing an executive for an international trip may vary slightly. You may want to download a few language converter apps to their phone or tablet before they leave. I also encourage you to research the customs and etiquette of the country your traveler is headed to and compile them into a document. It's also good to know the contact information for your country's embassy in the country your traveler will be visiting and the consulate locations in the cities on their itinerary. Include both the phone numbers and addresses on your traveler's itinerary. Do some research on the travel advisories for the specific areas they will be visiting. Finally, if you're sending your executive to a high-risk area of the world, you may need to do additional research on personal safety and best practices for that region. Your travel agent may also be able to help you with many of these things.

Keeping Your Executives Productive and Connected on the Road

One of the challenges of corporate travel is staying productive and connected to what's going on at the office while on the road. However, there are several things you can do to prepare your executive for being away from the office, and help them quickly get back into the swing of things upon their return.

Before the Trip

When you are prepping your executive for travel, these are some things you can do to get them ready.

- Create a travel folder (or poly envelope) for their travel details. This should include:

  ○ A printed copy of their detailed itinerary

  ○ Envelope(s) for travel receipts

  ○ Important meeting documents or agendas

  ○ For international travel, include doctors/dentists/hospitals recommended by your company health care plan in the countries being visited

 What I Use: See my favorite travel folder resources at **TheOrganizedAdmin.com**.

- Make sure their mobile office is packed. It should include:

  ○ A laptop

- ○ Portable devices (tablet, phone)

- ○ Cords (laptop, phone, tablet)

- ○ Power or A/V adapters

- ○ Flash drives

- ○ Mobile apps installed on the necessary device(s)

- ○ A three-outlet adapter plug (for sharing outlets at the airport)

- ○ Extra batteries

- ○ A small case with basic office supplies (mini stapler, paper clips, sticky notes, tape, rubber bands)

- Review the details of each meeting or presentation and include the appropriate handouts, speaking props, product samples, and business cards.

- Discuss how you can best assist your executive and keep him or her connected to what's happening at the office. Good communication with your executive is important when you're working side by side, but it's even more critical during travel. Does he prefer phone, email, or texting? What types of information does she want you to contact her about? Does he want summary updates or all of the details? Are you allowed to tell others why he is traveling or where? Are you supposed to scan her emails or will she check those on his own? For extended trips, do you need to scan/email his paper mail? Know their preferences before they leave so you can do everything possible to keep them connected and productive.

During the Trip

- When your executive is traveling, keep their travel itinerary with you at all times. This allows you to quickly troubleshoot any travel issues that may arise.

- While your executive is out of the office, be proactive about sorting their mail by priority for quick review when they return. Sort it into three stacks: important mail, marketing and industry publications, and junk mail. If appropriate, handle the junk mail yourself so they don't even have to bother with it.

- Help your executive get their filing caught up and assist with office/desk cleanup. Think about what would make the "re-entry" process as easy as possible when they return and take action on those items.

After the Trip

- If you sent your executive out the door with a travel folder and receipts envelope, retrieve that folder and envelope immediately! Are all receipts in there? Are the details you need for expense reports written on them? Are there any special details you need to know to process the expense report? Once you have all that information, process the expense report as soon as possible.

- Replenish any mobile office supplies that were consumed on the trip, such as batteries, office supplies, and business cards.

- Follow up on any emails, voice messages, updates, etc. that occurred while they were gone.

- Ask if everything worked well for this trip regarding flights, ground transportation, hotel, and amenities. Ask what, if anything, you need to adjust or change for the next trip. Then update your travel planning notes and pat yourself on the back for another travel planning success!

Handling Travel Delays, Cancellations, and Changes With Poise

Delays, cancellations, and last-minute changes are inevitabilities when it comes to organizing travel. You have to organize every detail as best as you can, then hope for a flawless trip. But I can tell you from my own travel experience that flawless trips are uncommon. So how do you prepare and maintain your sanity when chaos erupts?

One way is to research contingency options for travel delays or cancellations before you make the travel reservations. What are the alternative flight options for that day? How many flights are going in or out of the location your traveler is headed to? How far of a drive is it from the connecting airport to their final destination? How critical is it that your traveler get to their destination at the projected arrival time? Thinking through these questions as you research travel plans gives you some sense of the alternatives if things don't go as planned. Have a pre-departure conversation with your executive to go through potential options so you're both on the same page if something comes up.

Once your traveler is in transit, if a travel issue arises, enlist the help of your travel agent as soon as possible. Oftentimes I've been able to rebook my executive – with the assistance of my travel agent – as he stood in line at the airport ticket counter. We'd have him rebooked long before he ever reached the front of the line. This is important because the longer it takes to rebook a ticket, the fewer seats there are available on alternative flights. Tell your executives to call the travel agency directly if you want to be really efficient. It's truly the fastest and most effective way to get a traveler back enroute.

You can also troubleshoot travel snags by downloading relevant apps on your phone or tablet, as well as your executive's devices. Technology has made it very quick and simple to connect with car services, hotels, and airlines with the touch of your finger. Just make sure your devices and your executive's have the same apps – that way you both have the ability to quickly view updates or make changes to the itinerary during a trip.

When it comes to travel and travel planning, learning to go with the flow is the best advice I can offer you. Something will likely go wrong at some point, and your executive may verbalize ridiculous things to you over the phone. But stay calm and try to keep the situation from escalating. If you've applied the strategies in this chapter to plan, organize, and prepare your traveler, then you've done everything you could. Knowing this will help you to more easily separate your executive's frustration from feeling like it's a personal attack on you. Now you can focus on getting your executive calmed down and back on track.

PLAN OF ACTION:

☐ Find out if your company has a preferred travel agency or travel services provider that you should work with.

☐ If your company has one, schedule a meeting with the travel agency to learn more about how to work most effectively with them and use their online booking resources.

☐ If your company does not have an established travel provider, collect information from local agencies affiliated with national brands and interview them as potential travel providers.

☐ Familiarize yourself with your company's travel policies.

☐ Find out who the company's preferred travel providers are for hotels, airlines, car service, rental cars, etc.

☐ Develop your own standard and international travel forms, templates, and checklists to make your job easier.

☐ Visit **TheOrganizedAdmin.com** to download a travel itinerary template to get you started.

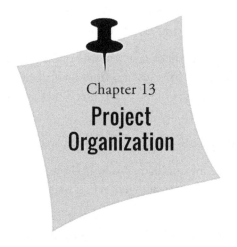

Chapter 13

Project
Organization

"Organization is what you do before you do something,
so that when you do it, it is not all mixed up."
~ A.A. MILNE, AUTHOR OF *WINNIE THE POOH*

We've already looked at applying the principles of organization to specific areas of your professional life, but many of the projects you work on are much more complex. One big project may include a series of smaller projects that you need to keep organized and moving forward. So how do you apply what you've learned to a multifaceted, complex application, such as project management?

Let's start by defining project management. It's planning, organizing, and managing resources to ensure the successful completion of specific project goals and objectives.

The systems involved in organizing projects may include any or all of the following: a project management tool, Outlook Tasks, spreadsheets, and documents. The type of project you're working on may dictate the specific tools you employ. In my experience, you do not need a fancy project management tool or complex Gantt charts to manage a project. You probably have everything you need right in front of you.

For example, if you're working on a self-assigned project, like creating your administrative procedures binder, you'll need a three-ring binder, some basic office supplies, a template for capturing your procedures, and a list of what you need to create to get it done. It's a pretty simple project that's easy to organize and maintain for the duration of the project.

If you're asked to work on a larger team project, though, the system will be much different. When I worked for an insurance company, I supported the team that developed life insurance policies for the banking industry. My team generated the products, created the marketing materials, put them through the compliance process, trained the sales team on selling them, and helped banks introduce the products once they were on the market. Every phase of this project involved intense organization to keep track of all of the components and where they were in the development and implementation process. At the time, project manager wasn't my job title, so I couldn't get access to project management software at my workstation. I had to use three-ring binders in combination with some detailed paper and digital forms and checklists to keep track of everything.

I had to apply the organization principles of gathering information, containing it, labeling it, and creating a home for it so that I, or anyone on my team, could find it. I had to create a system with my three-ring binders, paper files, and shared digital files that mirrored one another and made it easy to locate things. When ideas or action items were shared in meetings, they had to be captured so they could be completed. This project helped me develop some very detailed meeting planning forms and proofreading checklists to prevent important details from falling through the cracks. By applying these and other strategies I've talked about throughout this book, I was able to keep a very complex and unwieldy project running smoothly.

Fast-forward 18 years, and technology is much more accessible and user-friendly in helping manage big projects. I now use a combination of the techniques outlined here, along with a project management tool, to work with my team, collaborate, and stay on top of the details of the projects we're working on. When you have good systems in place that keep you organized, you can share the systems with others so they can follow them, too. It makes life at the office a lot less chaotic because the system provides the structure that underpins how you consistently get things done.

How Do You Organize a Project?

Some projects, especially big ones, can be overwhelming. The key is to break your project down into smaller pieces or tasks.

A few years ago, I created a Five-Day Challenge format to help assistants start creating their administrative procedures binder. Every time I do one of these challenges, my participants always end the challenge amazed at how much they accomplished in five short days – all while doing their regular jobs. The secret to their success is pretty simple: It's a combination of focus, accountability, support, and a time limit – all delivered to their inbox daily in the form of a plan of action! That's all project management is, when you think about it – it's a daily plan of action that keeps you moving toward your desired outcome.

When you're the project manager (whether it's in your job title or not), there are a few questions you need to answer to get things organized:

1. What is the project, and what is the desired outcome?

2. What is the timeline for completing this project?

3. Who is the project owner? (Note: This may be your executive, a colleague, or you. It's an important detail to define so you know who is responsible for key decisions that need to be made throughout the project.)

4. What are the steps or tasks required to achieve the desired outcome?

5. Who needs to be involved in planning for and completing the steps or tasks outlined?

6. What resources (money/budget, materials, software, etc.) are necessary to make it happen? For planning purposes, it's important to think through the costs that may be involved, what kind of resources may be required, and what type of support you need to make it happen.

7. Working backward from the targeted completion date, what are the start and due dates for each task? Assign a timeline to the individual action items. Depending on the size of your project, it's important to lay out the timing associated with each individual action item. This will help you set realistic expectations and keep you motivated throughout the process.

File Download: Download a template at **TheOrganizedAdmin.com** to help you start mapping out your plan.

Next, apply the strategies from this book to organize all the moving parts of your project:

- **Define your system for staying organized.** What do you need to create for checklists, forms, or templates to keep the various aspects of the project on track? What documents have you already created that you can modify for this specific project? Which software or project management tools will you use?

- **Organize your ideas.** Create a central location to capture your ideas, research, and tasks so you can refer to or add to them quickly. Choose a tool or location that allows you to collaborate with others on this project. Then write down every action that needs to be taken to complete the project. There are a lot of effective ways you can do this – whether it's a brain dump on a whiteboard, Word document, journal, or a digital notebook, or using mind-mapping software. Choose one and write down every single thing you can think of that needs to happen to complete your project. Then prioritize the tasks in the order they need to be completed.

- **Organize your workspace.** Assemble the supplies you need to keep the various project materials accessible and orderly for the duration of the project. Create a home on your desk or in a file drawer for these materials.

- **Organize your filing system.** Create the paper files and corresponding digital file folders so you can find what you need when you need it.

- **Organize your time.** Enter the tasks for your project into Outlook Tasks or your project management tool with start dates and due dates. Then schedule time on your calendar to complete the tasks. This is where admins often drop the ball. We know how long something should take under ideal conditions, but we never create – or schedule – the time to work on it and make it happen. It's also important to schedule time to manage and review the project as a whole – not just your individual tasks – so you don't lose sight of all of the moving parts of your project.

- **Organize your inbox.** Create folders and rules to help you manage the project correspondence effectively.

Here are a few other keys to helping you better manage your projects:

- Communicate regularly with your project's team members. Hold status meetings with the key stakeholders and people involved in the project. Track your progress – it will help with focus and accountability.

- Write down any challenges or roadblocks you encounter during the project and how you overcame them. This will help you think more clearly about the issues and avoid or overcome similar challenges in the future. Use your idea capture tool or project management software to keep a running list. If you can't think of any issues, dig a little deeper. There's almost always something you can improve next time.

- Celebrate the little achievements on the way to accomplishing your big project. They deserve recognition, and it will help maintain everyone's momentum and motivation. When you map out the project action items, identify the milestones that are worth celebrating. Then reward yourself and your team as you reach each one.

- If you're new to project management, find an accountability partner, mentor, or coach to encourage, support, and keep you on track. We all get by with a little (or a lot) of help from our friends, fellow admins, and colleagues. So don't overlook the impact a mentor can have. Choose someone who knows you well, provides objective feedback, and is willing to lend an ear or provide guidance.

Project management takes time, effort, and patience. There will be points when you have to stop and regroup on organizing aspects that have spun out of control. When this happens, look at your system. Identify what didn't work the way you intended. Make the adjustments and try again.

Using Technology to Work Virtually on Projects

A decade ago, almost everyone working on a project was typically located in the same building or on the same campus. Today, team members can be scattered across the globe or work from home. A lot of companies also employ subcontractors who aren't employees, yet are vital members of project teams. Learning how to work effectively on projects using virtual technologies is key to successfully managing projects. Choosing the ideal project management system that works with your environment – both from a technological and people perspective – is important, too.

If you're going to use a project management tool, it's important to look at some specific features and functionality before making a decision on the best tool for your project management needs. Remember: The technology should work for you, not the other way around.

- **Online/virtual accessibility:** Does it need to be accessible from one primary location or multiple locations? Is it accessible on mobile devices? Is it cloud-based or installed locally on your hard drive?

- **Integrated calendar/calendar syncing:** Does it need to sync with or connect to your calendar system? How easy is it to use?

- **Recurring tasks/task assignments:** Does it allow you to set up daily, weekly, or monthly recurring tasks? Can you assign tasks to others? Does it allow for comments and documents to be attached to a task?

- **Multi-project use:** How many projects can the tool support? Is there a central dashboard that will show you the status on all projects at once? Does it provide reporting functionality on completed tasks, late tasks, etc.?

- **Multiple users/user permission levels:** How many users can the tool support? Can you restrict access to read- or view-only? How easy is it to set up permission levels for users? Can you support internal employees and external contractors simultaneously?

- **File storing and sharing:** Does the tool allow you to upload and share documents? Where are these documents stored and maintained? If you want to maintain control of your documents on a secure network drive, how does document sharing work with this tool?

- **Wikis or digital notebooks:** Does the tool have a wiki or digital notebook component for capturing project notes, procedures, ideas, and research? How easy is it to use?

- **System notifications:** When a comment is added to a task or the task is completed, does the system notify you? Do those notifications come by email, or do you have to manually log into the tool to see updates? Can you reply to a system-generated notification and have your reply automatically added to the task comments?

- **Ease of system use:** How user-friendly is the tool? Read online reviews. Ask others for feedback. Watch as many demo videos and tutorials as you can.

One size does not fit all when it comes to project management tools. It depends upon your specific needs. And those needs may vary from project to project. So use these questions to poll your team, then research the available tools that might best fit your project management requirements. If possible, request a demo of the tool so you can see how it works firsthand. Then download a free trial of the software or tool you want to explore and test it out on a personal project first. This is a great way to test its user-friendliness and make sure it will do what you want it to do.

When you are comfortable with your selection, make a recommendation to your executive or IT department. You'll have a lot more credibility and confidence in making your recommendation if you've been using it and can share the pros and cons of the tools as it relates to the project management needs.

What I Use: To preview the project management tools I use, visit **TheOrganizedAdmin.com**.

Organizing projects takes a lot of time and focus because there are so many components to keep track of, but it's a very rewarding feeling when you organize the details, map out the plan, and see a project through to completion! Plus, adding project management skills to your resume will benefit you in just about every aspect of your career. So take a deep breath – and dive in!

PLAN OF ACTION:

☐ Think about a self-assigned project that you want to complete (e.g., administrative procedures binder, project management software research, or initiating a quarterly admin education lunch).

☐ Make a list of the organization systems and tools you need to complete the project (e.g., types of supplies, special software or apps, forms, and checklists).

☐ Create a plan for completing the project by breaking it down into the individual tasks involved and assigning start and due dates to each task.

☐ Enter each task with the start and due dates into your Outlook Tasks.

☐ Begin executing your plan.

☐ Now think about a more complex and involved project that you are working on. Using the above steps as your template, identify how you can better organize it. Implement your plan.

Part 4: Organizing Your Career

If you want to be ready for any change or opportunity at a moment's notice – planned or unplanned – then the most important area to apply the principles of organization is your own career! Let's look specifically at:

- Career Organization
- Beyond the Basic Job Search Toolkit

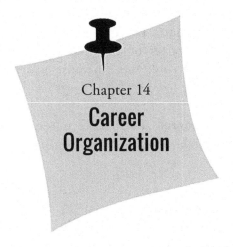

Chapter 14

Career Organization

"Security doesn't lie within a company. It lies within you."
~ JOAN BURGE, FOUNDER AND CEO, OFFICE DYNAMICS, INC.

rganization doesn't just apply to papers, projects, and things on your desk. You also have to be organized in how you approach your career if you want to achieve your goals and enjoy success.

I often receive emails from admins who lose their jobs unexpectedly. There was no advance warning. A merger, acquisition, downsizing, reorganization, or sudden exit of an executive may be to blame. But the end result is the same – the person is now looking for a job and is totally unprepared.

Unfortunately, many people in this situation haven't properly organized the documents and materials that support their career growth and development. They don't have an updated resume, a professional portfolio of work samples, or a social media presence.

This makes a stressful time even tenser. It also adds time to the job search because it's hard to start looking without the materials that support the search efforts. Don't let this happen to you!

Keeping your career organized is even more important than an organized workspace...because your livelihood depends on it.

Resource Alert: Take our career organization quiz at **TheOrganizedAdmin.com**.

Your Job Search Toolkit

Let's start with the items that are absolutely essential to helping you be prepared for any career change – expected or unexpected.

- Resume

- Cover letter

- Portfolio

- LinkedIn profile

- Personal business cards

Resume

A polished resume is one of the most powerful tools you have in your job search toolkit...if you put the time and effort into creating a positive professional representation of yourself.

Most admins have a resume, but not many consider it a living document. To be effective, you need to regularly update your resume with your most recent job responsibilities and achievements.

If you haven't updated your resume in the past three months, this is priority one. Make it a goal to update it before the end of next week. It doesn't have to be perfect, but it *does* need to be current. If you lose your job, then all you'll need to do is edit the material, rather than start from scratch. If a job promotion that requires an application comes along, you will need a current resume to submit on the spot. Not all job postings are listed for the same periods of time, so you have to be prepared to act quickly if you want to be considered for the opportunity.

If you don't have a resume, it's critical that you create one immediately. Start gathering the vital details required to get your resume created. You can go to your human resources department and ask to see your employee file so you can write down all of the job titles, dates, and salary details for each position you've held with your current company. Then you can work backward from there for other companies you've worked for.

Creating Multiple Versions of Your Resume

Ideally, you should have three versions of your resume: a master resume with everything in it, a formatted version for submission purposes, and a text version for the web or online job sites.

Your master resume file will contain all the details about your work history for your entire career. When you're updating your resume, update this master version so it's always current. You never know what information you'll need for job applications, and it's hard to go back and search for it later. It's also easy to forget important career details if you don't have it captured in this master document.

Once you have a master resume, you can create a customized and formatted version for each job you apply for. You should never submit the same version of your resume twice. Highlight your specific experience and accomplishments by how applicable they are to the position you're applying for. If you're applying for a job that requires a lot of travel planning or event planning, your experience in these areas should be the first bullets on your accomplishments list or job description section. It's also important to use the job posting's keywords in your resume. This will help prevent your resume and application from being screened out of the pile.

The third version of your resume is a text version of the customized version you create for each job. You may not need this every time, but many online job application tools can't read the formatting in a document, such as bold, italics, bullets on a list, lines, graphics, etc. You may need to create a version that looks good without the traditional formatting, which means keeping it plain, setting your bolded headlines off with brackets, and manually adding bullets using a dash or asterisk instead. If you can upload your resume as a PDF or Word attachment, you won't have to worry about this version.

Resource Alert: To see a sample of the text version of a formatted resume, visit **TheOrganizedAdmin.com**.

Resume Elements

Including a personal branding statement and solid career profile statement on your resume is another way to make an impression.

If you don't have these resume components, the following exercise will help you create them: *List the three words or short phrases that best describe the way you work, think, function, or perform professionally.*

These are the first three things you want your new potential employer to think when they hear your name. They are what people think of when your name is mentioned. They are your personal brand.

You're going to incorporate these personal branding components into your letterhead, business cards, references list, and cover letter. So spend some time thinking about who you are, what you do, and what you want people to think of you. Pull out your StrengthsFinder assessment or your personality type profile sheets and find the words or phrases from these documents that best describe you.

Examples:

Strategic thinker. Problem solver. Administrative professional.

Project manager. Event planner. Office professional.

Process analyst. Microsoft Office expert. Travel planning pro.

Businesspeople often refer to an "elevator pitch" when promoting their companies to someone who hasn't heard of them before. Your career profile statement is your personal elevator pitch. It's a brief, succinct statement of your professional experience and accomplishments that you can give to people you meet.

Examples: *(Note: Don't copy these — that's cheating! Use these models to create your own unique version!)*

Successful administrative professional with an established record for providing administrative support to multiple executives and their teams, acting as a liaison between employers and external business partners, coordinating office activities and schedules, and handling highly sensitive and confidential information in the corporate business environment.

A proactive and results-oriented administrative professional with a proven ability to provide comprehensive support for C- and VP-level executives and their management teams, a track record of exceeding expectations, and a knack for developing and maintaining administrative procedures that reduce redundancy, improve accuracy and efficiency, and achieve corporate objectives.

Dedicated, service-oriented professional with excellent communication and computer skills who has more than five years of experience providing legal support to corporate teams, acting as a liaison between multiple internal and external business partners, streamlining processes and procedures, and handling confidential information in the corporate environment.

Remember: Your resume should highlight your accomplishments with measurable results, not just duties performed for each job on your resume.

- Did you create procedures or streamline processes?

- Did you make something more efficient, and can you quantify the savings of money or time?

- Did you lead a project team or significantly contribute to one – even in a support role?

- Think about initiatives you took on without being asked and put them on paper!

Here are some examples to help you brainstorm:

- Implemented X, which reduced average processing time by X hours/days/weeks/months.

- Increased productivity by 15% by implementing X.

- Saved $1,000 in a 12-month period by doing X.

- Reduced customer complaint emails by X% by learning basic HTML so I could assist with basic website updates.

Other areas or experiences you may want to list on your resume include:

- Leadership positions

- Committee positions

- Professional organization memberships

- Specific software or hardware skills

- Honors or awards

- Specific areas of expertise

Resource Alert: Find some resume templates and excellent books on capturing attention with your resume, cover letter, and job search at **TheOrganizedAdmin.com.**

Cover Letter

Your cover letter is likely the first touch point you'll have with a potential employer, so it's extremely important to make the right impression. All admins should have two versions of their cover letter – a formal one that can be printed and an electronic version for online submission systems.

The content for both letters can be similar, but they shouldn't be identical. The formal letter should be longer and include more details since this is the one you'll likely submit to a potential employer. Your electronic version can be a bit more concise because employers' online job portals limit the size or number of words permitted for cover letters and resumes.

While the two versions of your cover letter will be slightly different, both should follow this basic structure:

- **First Paragraph – Introduction:** Explain who you are, why you are writing, and how you found out about the job.

- **Second Paragraph – Features:** Talk briefly about what you have to offer, and summarize your experience, qualifications, and skills, as well as their importance to the position you're seeking. Tie it into the job description and incorporate keywords used in the job listing to show that you fit what they are looking for.

- **Third Paragraph – Action:** Suggest the course of action you'd like the reader to take, such as schedule a phone call or interview. Also thank the person for their consideration.

Additionally, if you have a digital portfolio or a current LinkedIn profile, mention those things somewhere in your cover letter so the recruiter can preview your work samples and experience. You can include them in the body of your letter or at the end after your name and branding statements.

Professional Portfolio

How do you prove that you have the skills on your resume? What can you do to showcase these skills in a way that makes you stand out?

The answer is to create a professional portfolio.

Whether you are job hunting, going after a promotion, or simply want to document your career accomplishments, a professional portfolio will help you accomplish your objective!

If you don't already have a professional portfolio of work samples, I strongly encourage you to create one. Developing a professional portfolio will help you be remembered not only in an interview scenario, but at annual performance reviews as well.

A professional portfolio is a combination of work samples, educational background, and letters of recommendation that are compiled into a visually impactful package. It can include your:

- Resume

- Personality type or StrengthsFinder assessments

- Past performance reviews

- Forms

- Writing/communication samples

- Templates

- Checklists

- Project plans

- Before-and-after screenshots of databases you made more user-friendly or spreadsheets you formatted

- Procedures

- Graphics

- Websites

- Course agendas and certificates from continuing education

- Copies of diplomas or a relevant course syllabus or transcript (if applicable)

- Letters of recommendation

- Screenshots of LinkedIn recommendations

- Professional association memberships and leadership roles held (if applicable)

- Volunteer work

- Awards and recognitions

A professional portfolio can be presented in a variety of ways. One simple, professional option is a three-ring binder divided into sections. You can also create online or electronic versions to showcase your work via the Internet or other electronic means. Ultimately, it's a professional representation of you – it shows actual work product that you have completed.

Anyone can claim they have done something or have certain experience, but a real work sample with a brief explanation of what the project was, your role in it, and the final outcome is demonstrated proof. When you use a professional portfolio to document and showcase your skills, abilities, talents, and past performance, you will set yourself apart from the masses.

Resource Alert: Find resources to help you get started creating your professional portfolio at **TheOrganizedAdmin.com**.

LinkedIn Profile

With more than 400 million registered users worldwide (as of November 2015)[14], LinkedIn is one of the best social networking tools for admins. The site is a great online resume option and allows you to connect with other admins from around the world. It's also a great tool for organizing your career!

LinkedIn gives you the opportunity to network with people, including the HR team and executives at your current company, as well as companies and executives you'd like to work for. By forging relationships with these people now, you can get your foot in the door and name in front them. Then, when a job opportunity arises, your name will be a familiar one.

In addition to its career organization and networking benefits, LinkedIn is also great for building and establishing your personal brand, showcasing your expertise, and researching companies and industry trends.

Joining LinkedIn is free – all you have to do is sign up for an account and create a profile. However, it's important that you spend some time making sure your profile is polished and professional. If you're just getting started with LinkedIn, use these tips to create your profile:

1. **Upload a professional photo.** It doesn't have to be a professional headshot, but I strongly recommend one if you can get one. Avoid using photos that are overly personal, such as a vacation photo or family holiday picture.

2. **Highlight your experiences and education.** Your LinkedIn profile can double as a digital resume. However, for it to serve that purpose, you have to include elements from your resume – mainly your current and previous job experience and your educational background.

3. **Showcase your skills.** LinkedIn allows you to list your skills, as well as any honors or awards you've received. Don't pass up the opportunity to show off a little!

4. **Show your personality.** While LinkedIn is a professional social network, that doesn't mean your profile should be strictly corporate. Add some personal and professional interests to your profile. It will make you seem more like a real person and less like a resume. Use your personality type profile report or StrengthsFinder assessment to find keywords and descriptive phrases to include in your profile summary.

5. **Ask for recommendations and endorsements.** Once your LinkedIn profile is complete, ask your connections

to recommend or endorse you. This adds credibility to your skills, experience, and abilities.

LinkedIn is a great career organization tool that offers you a gateway to an expansive professional network, the ability to show off your career accomplishments, and a means for establishing an online professional presence. In our increasingly digital age, you can't afford not to take advantage of this free and useful professional tool.

Personal Business Cards

Many companies provide employees with their own business cards. However, if you want the ability to promote yourself professionally without the association of your current employer, personal business cards can go a long way in helping you represent yourself.

Personal business cards aren't just for job seekers – anyone who wants to make a professional impression can benefit from having their own cards. Personal business cards are a vital networking tool as they're a physical reminder of who you are, what you do, and how to get in touch with you.

The most crucial part of your business cards is your contact information, including your name, phone number, and email. However, you'll probably hand them out to people you don't know, so you may not want to include your address. Links to your social media profiles on LinkedIn, Twitter, and Facebook are great options for the back of your cards – as long as you're using them for professional purposes. You may also want to include your personal branding statement(s) and a link to your digital professional portfolio if you have one.

Printing your cards is fairly simple, and can easily be done at home with your own printer or at your local copy store. There are also several online companies that offer inexpensive business cards if you prefer not to print them yourself.

What I Use: To create and print your own business cards, check out a few of my favorite tools and resources at **TheOrganizedAdmin.com**.

Don't show up to any professional event without a business card! Doing so can mean missed opportunities, lost connections, and potentially even losing out on a dream job. Create some personal business cards so you don't miss out on a single chance to make a lasting first impression!

Create Your Job Search Toolkit

Every single one of us is one business decision away from having our professional lives turned upside down. But you can take control of the situation more quickly if your career toolkit is complete, current, and includes all the items you need to quickly activate your network and transition yourself into a different company or position. Your job search toolkit contains key career components that help you proactively weather the business decisions you least expect!

PLAN OF ACTION:

☐ Find your resume and update it. Do it today, if possible. If not, schedule it for some time this week.

☐ Update or create your professional portfolio of work samples. Begin by gathering work samples you may want to include.

☐ Update or create your LinkedIn profile.

☐ Download the personal business card template at **TheOrganizedAdmin.com** and create your own personalized business cards.

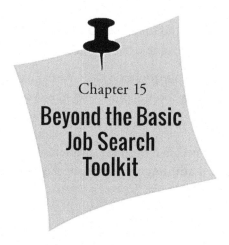

Chapter 15

Beyond the Basic Job Search Toolkit

"I never dreamed about success. I worked for it."
~ Estée Lauder

So far, we've talked about some of the basics you need to organize your admin career. But in our profession, the basics are rarely good enough. You need to go beyond the basics and equip yourself with the advanced resources you need to be successful.

Now that you have the essentials down, let's explore some of the more advanced components of organizing yourself for career changes – both the expected and the unexpected.

Digital Portfolio

A digital professional portfolio is a collection of work samples, training/education certificates, and other materials (such as a resume and letters of recommendation) that demonstrates your professional experience and skills in a dynamic, online format. It's a professional representation of you that shows actual work you have completed and provides proof of your on-the-job performance, abilities, skills, awards, and accomplishments. It's also a great tool for organizing your admin career!

There's no right or wrong recipe for the perfect portfolio, but the most dynamic ones usually include a variety of text, photos, graphics, downloadable files, and video/audio components that lend credibility to your career accomplishments in a way a resume alone can't.

Creating a digital portfolio doesn't require a degree in computer science or significant web development knowledge. There are several free tools you can use. My favorite is WordPress – a simple, easy-to-use (and free) online platform that helps you get a portfolio up and working very quickly.

 Resource Alert: Find additional resources to help you create your digital portfolio at **TheOrganizedAdmin.com**.

Items to Include in Your Digital Portfolio

The ultimate goal of a digital portfolio is to showcase your skills and background. It can also act as a platform for boosting your professional visibility online. To achieve both of these objectives, you need to include a dynamic set of materials that demonstrate your talents and drive people to your portfolio. Some materials you can include are:

- Introductions for the portfolio

- Bio

- Resume

- Work samples

- Social media profile links

- A link to your blog

As with anything online, there are always personal safety and security issues to consider when building your digital portfolio. Keep in mind, once you put something on the Internet, you can never completely remove it. Copies of website pages are stored on servers around the world, so you cannot control where that information may be saved or retrieved even after you delete it. Here are some guidelines to follow when determining what to include and what to leave out of your digital portfolio:

- Don't include personal data, such as your home address or phone number. If you want to include a phone number, set up a free Google Voice number.

- Create an email address to use only for digital portfolio contact purposes. Or use a contact form on your site instead.

- Depending on the companies you've worked for and the type of work you have done, you may want to remove specific information about the location and/or dates for personal safety reasons.

- Add a subtitle to the top of your resume that says "Online Resume" to indicate it may not contain the same level of detail as your print resume. If that's the case, add a note that a more detailed version of your resume is available upon request, and link the note to your contact form on your digital portfolio site.

- Remove specific dates from your educational background if you think it may reveal your age. You only need to list the highest degree you have attained.

- Don't post confidential information regarding current or past employers or projects you've worked on while employed there.

- Use a professional headshot. If you don't have one, use an image that's not overly personal and includes only you. Don't include family members or vacation pictures on your digital portfolio.

Professional Network

If you haven't been developing and nurturing your professional network, now is the time to start! Your network is a valuable resource, whether you're looking for a new opportunity, you're out of work, or just want to expand your professional reach.

There are three primary ways to build and nurture your professional network: face to face, online, and via a personal advisory board.

Don't let the word "networking" scare you off. You don't have to be an overly extroverted person to be a successful networker. To me, networking isn't something you do; networking is a mindset. It's making connections between people and resources and being able to connect yourself or others to those people or resources when you need them.

Don't think about it from the perspective of what others can do for you. Instead, think about what you can do for others. Practice networking from the mindset of giving to others, connecting them to resources, and helping them.

I recognize that face-to-face networking can make some people uncomfortable, especially if you are introverted by nature. But you can't hide behind your computer and expect to advance in your career. You have to get out and connect with people in person.

However, you shouldn't overlook online networking either. There seem to be two extremes with online networking – those who dive in full-force and those who avoid it like the plague. You need a healthy mix. It's not mandatory that you're on every social network. In fact, if you only choose only one, pick LinkedIn. It's more than sufficient to build your professional network socially.

Another networking strategy is to develop your personal advisory board. Your board is a small group of objective people who know you well, are interested in your success, and are able to help you think more clearly. They accelerate your professional success and take some of the fear and uncertainty out of working through big decisions or evaluating opportunities.

Your personal advisory board can include coworkers, colleagues, members of professional associations, friends, people you follow on the web, or even family members. The key is to think about who inspires you to view things in different ways. Who challenges you to pursue new opportunities? These are probably some people you should consider spending more time with either in person or virtually. Keep in mind, you don't have to tell them they're on your personal advisory board. What's important here is that you know who sits at your virtual boardroom table when you need counsel and support.

Interview Preparation

You landed an interview at a company you'd love to work for... so now what?

To ace an interview, you need to be as prepared as possible, and that means doing two crucial things.

First, practice your interview techniques. Find a friend or family member who can ask you questions until you get comfortable responding. And make sure you have a polished response to this important one: Why are you looking for a new position and/or leaving your current company? You have to be able to answer this question positively without faltering or being frazzled. Until you can do that, you're going to struggle with the interview. Once you're comfortable answering potential interview questions, practice over and over again. I recommend practicing in front of a mirror so you can see how your body and facial expressions look to others when you're sitting in front of them. And I also recommend practicing your interview skills via video chat with a friend using the webcam on your computer. If you can, record yourself and watch it so you're aware of how your facial expressions and mannerisms are seen from the other side. More companies are doing initial interviews by video conference, so you need to be prepared when it happens to you.

Second, do your homework on the company you're interviewing with. Read the latest earnings report, blog posts, and press releases. Research the company's culture, and figure out how your skills and abilities fit in with it. Remember, an interview is a two-way street. You need to be prepared to ask and answer questions. What do you need to know about the position and company to make a decision about whether you want to work there? Ask the interviewer these questions.

In addition to company-specific questions, the following are some great questions for admins to ask during an interview:

1. How long have you worked here? What do you enjoy and value most about the company?

2. How many assistants have supported you during your career? Who was the best? Worst? Why?

3. Why is this position open? How often has it been filled in the past five years? How has it evolved in that time? *(If the position has had a lot of turnover, ask why they think this has been the case.)*

4. What are the department's strengths and weaknesses? Where do you see this position adding the most value?

5. What was it about my resume that caught your eye and made you call me for an interview?

6. How do you determine or evaluate success for the person in this position? What are the key things this position needs to accomplish in the first three to six months of employment? *(If you really want to impress them, walk into the interview with your own 30-, 60-, or 90-day plan. Let them know what you intend to do to get up to speed and fully integrated into the team and company culture.)*

7. Who or what will be my biggest challenge in this position? Why? *(If there is more than one person in the interview, watch their exchange of glances or facial expressions when you ask this. You'll be able to tell if underlying issues are lurking.)*

8. How do you view the administrative support role in the overall functioning of this office? *(If they view the role as the person who makes the coffee, sorts the mail, and is mostly clerical, then it might not be the best career move. If the role is viewed as the hub of the wheel that keeps things running smoothly, facilitates project and communication flow, and is a vital role to the team's success, then it might be a good fit.)*

9. What is the typical workweek like for this position? Is overtime expected? How often?

10. How many executives in this company commute from another state on a weekly basis? *(I've learned this may indicate they don't have families to go home to in the evenings and are more likely to spend longer hours at the office each day. This impacts the hours required of their assistant at the office as a result.)*

11. What makes a great first impression? How do you make a good first impression? *(You can learn a lot about a person's viewpoint with this one. It can also help you learn about their future expectations of you.)*

12. What are the connectivity expectations for this position? Does this position need to be connected to email and the office 24/7? *(This can be an important piece of information to have before you begin negotiating salary and benefits if the position is offered to you.)*

13. What do you think is the greatest opportunity facing the organization (or department) in the near future? Biggest threat?

14. What are the first projects this position will be working on? What would I need to do to get up to speed on them as soon as possible?

15. Do you have any hesitation about my qualifications for this position? *(If you think you would like the job and working for the company, you need to find out what else you can do to seal the deal. If they have hesitations, be prepared to discuss them. Going into the interview with your professional portfolio can help you fill in any gaps and answer questions with work samples and proof that you can do what you say you can do.)*

Each interview is a unique experience. Some interviewers will volunteer details about the company, the position, and the culture that may give you the insight you need without having to ask. Other situations will require you ask. It's important to prioritize your questions so you get the vital information you need to make a good decision. It's also important to assess each interview environment and determine how engaged the interviewer is in the conversation so you know when to bring things to a close. If you're called back for another interview, you may have additional opportunities to ask more questions.

If and when you're approached about a new position or job, make sure to review your interview questions and tailor or add to them as necessary. Interviewers want to see someone engaged in their profession and what's going on around them. Asking questions during an interview is a great way to find out the information you need to make an educated and informed decision if the job or position is offered to you.

References

To be organized in your admin career, it's important to have a list of three to five references that you – or a prospective employer – can call on to give feedback about your professional experience, skills, and performance.

This list should include the name, email address, and phone number for each reference. You may also want to include a note about your relationship with them, such as "The executive I supported for (number) years at (company)."

Make sure that you ask each person if he or she is willing to speak about your working relationship. You should also tell your references when you apply for a position, and with what company, so they can be prepared for the call or email. Finally, tell them which skills, abilities, etc., that you want them to highlight, if applicable. You don't want to leave your references' recommendations to chance – so make sure they're prepared!

Annual Performance Review Prep

Performance reviews aren't something a lot of people look forward to. They can be uncomfortable, stressful, and time-consuming to prepare for. However, a critique of your job performance during the past six to 12 months doesn't have to be painful. It's actually a great opportunity to show your executive and employer the value you bring to the company, your commitment to your career, and your dedication to being an admin.

Acing your review is fairly easy to do – if you proactively prepare for it. Here are some tips for getting yourself ready:

- **Create or update your professional portfolio.** As I mentioned earlier, one of the best ways to showcase your professional experience, skills, work samples, and talents to your employer is with a professional portfolio. If you don't already have one, it's important that you start creating yours today! If you already have one, make sure to continuously update it throughout the year so you're not rushing to update it right before your review.

- **Track your tasks and accomplishments.** Create a list of your weekly tasks and accomplishments and save it to your desktop. As you complete new tasks each week – regardless of how big or small – add them to this list. This will allow you to provide your executive with a comprehensive list of your professional accomplishments and highlights of your ongoing responsibilities come review time. This list can also come in handy when creating or updating your professional portfolio. It's especially useful if you're presented with a new job opportunity – whether it's expected or unexpected!

- **Network, network, network.** I talk to so many admins who underestimate the power of a network. Your current colleagues can be some of the most valuable in your network. Taking the time to get to know the people you work with allows you to know whom to turn to with specific questions, both inside and outside of your department. These intraoffice ties also demonstrate your commitment to collaboration within the workplace and your ability to be a team player – both of which will be important when your review rolls around.

- **Know what's expected and go beyond it.** To earn a stellar performance review, you need to fully understand what's expected of you. Make sure you understand everything your job entails. If there's any question about tasks or responsibilities, ask your executive for clarification. Don't wait until your performance review to find out that you're missing the mark on something.

Create a Strategic Career Plan

The last component of your admin toolkit that we need to address is your strategic career plan. Do you have one in place? Do you know how to get one started?

A strategic career plan is a combination of your personal vision, mission, and goals used to guide your professional growth and development. Once created, your plan will help you evaluate yourself and determine where your career is headed. It will also help you understand where you are right now and identify what you need to do to get to the next step on your career path. The exercise of creating and maintaining your plan allows you to shift from a reactive approach to a proactive approach in managing your career development.

Everyone has their own unique purpose and calling in the admin profession, and no two paths will be the same. This is why it's crucial that you create a career plan that's tailored specifically to you. It needs to reflect your personality, strengths, passions, interests, and career goals, as it will be your guide in making decisions about training opportunities, skills development, new positions, performance review goals, and more!

You can include whatever you'd like in your career plan. However, there are three important questions you need to answer in order for your plan to be effective.

- **Where are you now?** To determine where you are now, write down the goals you've already achieved. How did you tackle these goals and what made you successful? What goals did you fail to achieve and why? Is there anything you're tolerating instead of overcoming? What's your mission or the impact you want to have?

 What I Use: Check out my all-time favorite tool for creating a personal mission statement at **TheOrganizedAdmin.com**.

- **Where do you want to go?** There's a world of possibilities out there, so picking a path can be a challenge. The good news is that this plan isn't set in stone. It can, and should, evolve as you gain more skills and experience. Ask yourself why you chose to be an admin. What factors are critical to your success? What is your specialty or niche?

- **How are you going to get there?** Think about your short-term (next year), mid-range (two to three years), and long-term (five years and beyond) career goals. What does your career look like at each of these points? Keep in mind, you'll never be greater than your most lofty ambition. So don't sell yourself short. Write down all the things you need to do to get where you want to be. Include certifications, education, training, and mentoring that you will need. Document any projects that you need to complete, such as a professional portfolio, and list publications or books you should read.

Go through each of these questions and compile your answers to each into some form of documentation, whether it's a Word file or handwritten notes in a notebook. Then review your notes and look at your long-term objectives. Begin creating specific goals that you want to achieve in the next 12 months that will help you advance toward those larger objectives. To hold yourself accountable in achieving each goal, break it down into specific steps or tasks involved in making it happen. Brainstorm the resources – materials and money – required to complete it. Identify a targeted completion date. Add it to your calendar. Then write down the actual date you accomplished it so you have a written record of your achievements and the progress you are making toward reaching your goals.

File Download: Download a career-planning template at **TheOrganizedAdmin.com**.

When you take this approach, your strategic career plan becomes a literal plan of action that keeps you on track and accountable. It also becomes a fantastic tool for discussing your goals and accomplishments over the course of the year with your executive during one-on-one meetings and at annual performance review time. It also helps you make better decisions about the opportunities and challenges you face along the way!

Better prepare yourself for career opportunities and take your admin toolkit to the next level by creating and incorporating these elements. It will take some extra time, but think of it as an investment in yourself and your admin career!

PLAN OF ACTION:

☐ Research the online tools available for creating the digital edition of your professional portfolio.

☐ Decide which tool you'd like to use for your digital portfolio and use it to begin developing yours.

☐ Review your professional networking activities and identify one way you can improve your networking efforts.

☐ Begin an interview questions list in your journal or professional portfolio. Continue adding ideas to it so you have a list to refer to when needed.

☐ Develop a list of three to five references and include their names, emails, phone numbers, and what your working relationship was with them.

☐ Create an accomplishments list document, and add to it each week throughout the year so you are better prepared for your annual performance review.

☐ Develop a strategic administrative career plan for yourself.

Part 5: Putting It All Together

We're almost done! Here are a few final tips and resources to help you put it all together:

- Calling In the Experts

- Putting It All Together – Your Plan of Action as The Organized Admin

- Appendix Resources

Chapter 16

Calling In the Experts

"Be strong enough to stand alone, smart enough to know when you need help, and brave enough to ask for it."
~ UNKNOWN

If you're feeling overwhelmed at the prospect of getting organized, or want some help getting started, don't be afraid to ask for help or even hire a professional organizer. There's no shame in getting a little assistance with such a big and important organization task. A pro can help you get from point A to point B much more quickly than if you do it on your own. They can also show you how to get things done more efficiently and be more effective in managing your assignments.

I remember the first time I told someone I hired a professional organizer to help me with my home office. They were in shock. "But you're one of the most organized people I know!" they exclaimed. "Why do you need a professional organizer?" My answer is that what you do for others and what you're willing to do or have time to do for yourself can be two very different things.

I've always been very organized, and I've worked with a lot of managers and executives who required me to be organized. So I was genuinely surprised by how much I learned and benefited from working with a professional organizer. Let me explain.

A professional organizer is much more than an organizer. The truly qualified and talented professional organizers are efficiency experts. They help you lay out your workspace and office properly. They show you how to implement systems for processing daily work and project requests. Many can even coach you to better utilize technology to organize your time, projects, and email. No matter how organized you are, you can always improve your efficiency. If you keep an open mind, an objective perspective will help you identify ways to improve how you work.

Working with a professional organizer isn't just about creating files and removing piles from your space. It's about developing systems and processes that fit with how you work so you can stay organized and maximize your productivity. It's about creating homes for things so you can put them away and know where they are the next time you need them. A professional organizer can also help you speed up the organization process. If someone helps you reason through where to file something, or whether you need it at all, you make decisions quicker. Clutter can be overwhelming and downright depressing! It's vital to have someone to encourage you as you plow through the piles and help you get past the emotional and mental issues associated with the clutter.

Another benefit of a professional organizer is that he or she makes it easier to identify your organization trouble spots, especially when it comes to organizing your workspace. I'm a saver.

I like to read things on paper instead of on the computer. So I maintain a lot of information in my home office for reference, and it catches up with me if I don't stay on top of it. Working with my professional organizer helped me identify some of my bad habits and develop strategies for overcoming them. It also saved me money because I probably would have argued that I needed more file space when what I truly needed was a better system for paper management.

A professional organizer provides tactics and strategies for working more effectively with chronically disorganized or ADHD co-workers. You may joke about this with your team members, but these are legitimate issues for some people – and it impacts how they work and how you work with them. Look for a professional organizer who is certified by the Institute for Challenging Disorganization or the National Association of Professional Organizers in these areas. This just might be the light bulb moment you've been waiting for in learning how to work better with your executive and team members.

If a professional organizer sounds like the solution to your workspace chaos, the next step is to gain your executive's support for hiring a professional organizer. To make your case, you'll need to demonstrate how the expense of an organizer is worth the investment. These are some of the points you can make when discussing the subject with your executive:

- Refer to the professional organizer as a productivity or efficiency expert.

- Document all of the areas or situations where you feel you could be more productive, but need additional support in getting past roadblocks.

- Do your research and give your executive the facts and figures on the amount of time and money saved and the increased productivity that an organized and efficient workplace can provide. A professional organizer can give you some of these stats. The National Association of Professional Organizers website, NAPO.net, is a great resource, too.

- Be willing to pay for the first session or two yourself. Then document the improvements and systems that you've implemented so your executive can see the tangible results. This may inspire them to fund future sessions and reimburse you for the past sessions you paid for yourself. Either way, the personal investment is worth it!

Once you have approval to hire a professional organizer – or you make the investment to pay for one yourself – you need to keep an eye out for these things as you interview organizers:

- Look for a Certified Professional Organizer.

- Find one who is a member of the NAPO.

- Ask for references or referrals.

- Meet with the person for a consultation and/or talk to them by phone.

- Do Internet research and see who others recommend.

We're all being asked to do more with less. A professional organizer can help you squeeze more time from your day, improve productivity in your office, and give you strategies you can apply everywhere to help you fast-track your progress with built in accountability. Plus, you'll look like the office superstar yet again!

PLAN OF ACTION:

☐ Research and interview professional organizers in your area.

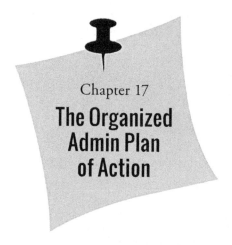

Chapter 17
The Organized Admin Plan of Action

"The secret to change is to focus all of your energy not on fighting the old, but on building the new."
~ Socrates

To become The Organized Admin, you must identify your time style and space style to develop simple systems to create an organized life that works for you. Getting organized is not a destination or a static state that remains simply because you got there once. It requires a change in habits and thinking in combination with a systematized approach to maintain organization over time.

Once you have identified where you need better habits and simple systems, you must invest time in creating those systems and finding the tools that work the most optimally for you. When you get them created and tested, and you know they work for you, then you have to use them religiously. That's how you learn to trust your systems. You have to put the effort in to changing your habits and implementing those systems that will help you get organized! Trust me. It takes time and some trial and error to get it right, but it is worth the effort!

You also have to remain open to modifying your systems when situations change, responsibilities shift, or you find yourself facing a new organizing challenge. Perhaps you just got promoted and new responsibilities were given to you. This may require learning how to manage larger projects with more complexity. If your company goes through a merger or acquisition, entire culture shifts may occur that force you to work differently than you did previously. If you go through a significant personal transition of any sort, it can shift your priorities and the way you work going forward. These types of situations require a careful review of your systems and identifying what you need to adjust to ensure continued success in staying organized for the long haul.

Handling Situational Disorganization

There's also this thing called situational disorganization. It happens to even the most organized people. It occurs when life strikes unexpectedly, and you find yourself thrust into a new situation that upsets the systems and habits you normally employ to stay on top of things. It may be a move, an illness, a change in workload, or a new job. During these times of transition, you can expect a certain amount of clutter, chaos, and disorganization to occur. It's not permanent, but it can be disruptive and frustrating if you aren't prepared for the effect it has on your organization. It happened to me as I was trying to write this book.

My husband was offered a new job two states away from where we lived, and suddenly my life erupted into chaos. I needed to keep my business running, finish this book, and coordinate travel for speaking engagements – all while trying to get a house put on the market for sale, pack up my husband so he could start his new job a few weeks before we moved, and coordinate the packing, loading, and transfer of our stuff!

I love an organizing challenge. And I love organizing moves – personal or corporate. So the move was orchestrated about as flawlessly as possible. But working on my book, keeping my inbox clean, and keeping my home office organized so I could continue working was a disaster! I felt like a total failure, especially since I was writing a book on getting organized. I couldn't even keep myself organized!

That was when my business coach, Maggie, reminded me that this was temporary. "This is called situational disorganization," she said one day. And she was right. It took a few months for me to get myself back on track. But I did. The situation passed, and I implemented many of my previous systems in my new office with the same success as before. I also had a chance to review and refresh some things that were different about working in my new space. I took advantage of this opportunity to tweak a few things to make them work better for me moving forward.

Dealing With System Failures

We all know how quickly things can change. You may find yourself struggling with a new aspect of organization that you had a good system for, but now it's just not working. This happens. When you notice the tension and frustration building, don't abandon the system entirely. Pause and look more closely at what isn't working. Sometimes, having someone else help you troubleshoot your system makes it easier to pinpoint and resolve the problem.

This is where I've found working with a professional organizer to be immensely valuable. Organizers have expertise in the areas that can help resolve issues much more efficiently and quickly than struggling through it by yourself.

You Can Do It!

You can become more organized if you make the conscious choice to do so. The process of getting organized takes time, patience, and a willingness to change. My goal in writing this book was to give you ideas and action plans for organizing key areas that assistants struggle with. You may need to tweak some of these strategies to make them work for you. But you don't have to start from scratch in figuring it out. The framework for what you need to get started is all right here.

Throughout this book, I've outlined simple plans of action to help you think through and implement the ideas shared in each chapter. If you're trying to get organized, and you're struggling with where to begin, read the first five chapters to get an overview of the principles and strategies that help you get organized. Then pick a chapter (from six through 15) each month for the next year and make it part of your professional development goals. One chapter at a time isn't overwhelming. It will help you focus on forming the new habits you need within a reasonable timeframe. The plans of action included with each chapter will help.

So, what are you waiting for? If you want to be successful as an administrative professional, you have to be organized. Leverage your unique organizing style to create systems, reduce overwhelm, increase productivity, and become The Organized Admin!

Appendix

RECOMMENDED READING

Best Practices for Administrative Professionals

- *Administrative Excellence* by Erin O'Hara Meyer

- *Be the Ultimate Assistant* by Bonnie Low-Kramen

- *Become An Inner Circle Assistant* by Joan Burge

- *Executive Secretary Magazine* published by Marcham Publishing, Lucy Brazier, CEO

- *Not "Just An Admin!"* by Peggy Vasquez

- *The Definitive Personal Assistant & Secretarial Handbook* by Sue France

Communication, Career Planning, and Success

- *Crucial Conversations* by Patterson, Grenny, McMillan and Switzler

- *Eat, Drink & Succeed* by Laura Schwartz

- *Guerilla Marketing for Job Hunters 3.0* by Jay Conrad Levinson

- *The 7 Habits of Highly Effective People* by Stephen R. Covey

- *The 8th Habit: From Effectiveness to Greatness* by Stephen R. Covey

Email Management

- *Brilliant Email* by Dr. Monica Seeley

- *Inbox Detox* by Marsha Egan

- *The Executive Secretary Guide to Taking Control of Your Inbox* by Dr. Monica Seeley

Developing New Habits and Navigating Change

- *Better Than Before* by Gretchen Rubin

- *Change Anything: The New Science of Personal Success* by Patterson, Grenny, Maxfield, McMillan, and Switzler

- *The First 30 Days* by Ariane de Bonvoisin

Organizing Tips and Ideas

- *2 Minute Organizing Miracles* by Becky Esker

- *Clutter Control!* by Susan Wright

- *Confessions of an Organized Homemaker* by Deniece Schofield

- *Keeping Work Simple* by Carol Cartaino and Don Aslett

- *The One-Minute Organizer Plain & Simple* by Donna Smallin

- *The TSSI Style Guide: A Professional's Resource* by Cena Block

Productivity and Time Management

- *Doing the Right Things Right* by Laura Stack
- *Leave the Office Earlier* by Laura Stack
- *No Excuses!* by Brian Tracy
- *SuperCompetent* by Laura Stack
- *What To Do When There's Too Much To Do* by Laura Stack

Strengths, Personality Type, and Work Styles

- *Fascinate* by Sally Hogshead
- *StandOut* by Marcus Buckingham
- *StrengthsFinder 2.0* by Tom Rath
- *Type Talk* by Otto Kroeger
- *Type Talk at Work* by Otto Kroeger
- *The Art of SpeedReading People* by Paul D. Tieger
- *The Birth Order Book* by Dr. Kevin Leman

Travel Planning

- *Kiss, Bow, or Shake Hands* by Terri Morrison and Wayne A. Conaway

Technology Training

- *100 Tips Using MacOS X & Office 2011* (Spiral-bound Guide) by Vickie Sokol Evans, MCT

- *100 Tips Using Windows 8.1 & Office 2013* (Spiral-bound Guide) by Vickie Sokol Evans, MCT

RESOURCES FOR THE ORGANIZED ADMIN

Certifications

- Certified Administrative Professional – IAAP-HQ.org

- World Class Assistant Certification – OfficeDynamics. com

- Microsoft Office Certifications – Microsoft.com/en-us/ learning/office-certification.aspx

- Advanced Certificate for the Executive Personal Assistant – BMTG.org

- Certified Professional Organizer – NAPO.net

- The Institute for Challenging Disorganization provides five levels of certificates and certification. ChallengingDisorganization.org

- Project Management Professional – PMI.org

- Certified Associate in Project Management – PMI.org

- Certified Meeting Professional – ConventionIndustry.org

Organizing and Productivity Websites

- ABowlFullofLemons.net

- ChallengingDisorganization.org

- GetOrganizedNow.com

- GetOrganizedWizard.com

- GettingThingsDone.com

- InnovativelyOrganized.com

- JulieMorgenstern.com

- NAPO.net

- OrganizingHomeLife.com

- OrgJunkie.com

- PeterWalshDesign.com

- SaneSpaces.com

- TheOrganizedAdmin.com

- TheProductivityPro.com

Visit **TheOrganizedAdmin.com** to see our most current list of resources for apps, software, organizing supplies, and more.

OTHER BOOKS BY JULIE PERRINE

The Innovative Admin: Unleash the Power of Innovation In Your Administrative Career

TheInnovativeAdmin.com

5 Simple Steps to Creating Your Administrative Procedures Binder (e-book)

Your Career Edge: Create a Powerful Professional Portfolio (e-book)

Your Career Edge: Create a Professional Online Portfolio (e-book)

PRODUCTS AND TRAINING FROM ALL THINGS ADMIN

Administrative Procedures Toolkit

AdminPro Training Series

AdminTech Crash Course

Creating a Powerful Professional Portfolio

Kick-Start Creating Your Administrative Procedures Binder

Myers-Briggs Type Indicator Personality Assessments

Professional Portfolio Builder

Boost Your Professional Visibility With An Online Portfolio

Strategic Career Planning

Template Packages

Travel Planning

Training On Demand

Visit **AllThingsAdmin.com** for information on these products and many more.

About the Author

Julie Perrine

Certified Administrative Professional® – Organizational Management
Certified Myers-Briggs Type Indicator® Administrator
Certified Productivity Pro® Consultant

Julie Perrine, CAP-OM, is an administrative expert, trainer, motivational speaker, and author. She is the founder and CEO of All Things Admin, a company dedicated to developing and providing innovative products, training, mentoring, and resources for administrative professionals.

Julie has more than 20 years of experience in the administrative profession spanning several industries and serving in corporate and startup settings. Her mission is to guide, encourage, and connect administrative professionals to the technologies, ideas, resources, and people they need to achieve professional success. Her upbeat, straightforward approach to handling opportunities and challenges gives admins proactive strategies for developing a plan, making progress, and achieving results.

Julie has created several innovative tools and programs for administrative professionals, including the Administrative Procedures Toolkit, Kick-Start Creating Your Administrative Procedures Binder Course, Professional Portfolio Builder, and eP-ortfolio Builder. Julie's first book, *The Innovative Admin: Unleash the Power of Innovation In Your Administrative Career,* was released in 2012. She is also the author of the eBooks: *5 Simple Steps to Creating Your Administrative Procedures Binder, Your Career Edge: Create a Powerful Professional Portfolio,* and *Your Career Edge: Create a Professional Online Portfolio.*

Julie transformed a career as an administrative professional into several successful enterprises and shares her knowledge, expertise, and resources with individuals, corporations, and organizations as an online business model consultant, personality type strategist, and productivity expert.

Julie writes regularly for the Executive Secretary Magazine and All Things Admin, and her articles have been published in professional publications worldwide. She has been active in local and international organizations, including the International Association of Administrative Professionals and the National Association of Professional Organizers.

To inquire about having Julie Perrine speak at your next meeting, contact us through our website at **AllThingsAdmin.com**.

Connect With All Things Admin

Website
AllThingsAdmin.com

Facebook
Facebook.com/AllThingsAdmin

Twitter
Twitter.com/JuliePerrine
Twitter.com/ProceduresPro

LinkedIn
LinkedIn.com/company/All-Things-Admin
LinkedIn.com/in/JuliePerrine

For downloadable resources mentioned in this book, visit
TheOrganizedAdmin.com.

To inquire about having Julie Perrine speak at your next meeting, contact us through our website at AllThingsAdmin.com.

Acknowledgements

Behind every published author is a community of people that were essential to the completion of the project. I am very blessed to have such a dedicated and enthusiastic support team encouraging me on this journey.

It is with deep gratitude that I express my thanks and appreciation to the following people for their specific contributions:

- To my best friend and Chief Encouragement Officer – my husband, Todd. Attempting to write a book and making a major move in the same year might not have been the most ideal timing, but we did it! Flexibility, a sense of humor, and most importantly, organization, were the keys to our success. Thanks for letting me help you organize your new office!

- To my professional organizer, business coach, move mentor, and friend, Maggie Jackson. Since we started working together many years ago, you've been one of my biggest supporters personally and professionally. Thank you for your encouragement, guidance, and accountability check-ins throughout the writing process. Who knew you'd become my move mentor as well when we started this journey? I can't imagine having done either without you.

- To the creator of the Time & Space Style Inventory, Cena Block. I'm so glad our paths crossed when they did. Your expertise on organizing styles have made this book better. Thank you for being a willing collaborator!

- To my team and their team members – Suzanne Bird-Harris, Amber Miller, Christine Morris, Michelle Witten, Ruth Pierce, Penny Sailer, and Claire Wenisch. You are my A-Team! I'd be lost without you. Thank you for sticking with me through it all.

- To my graphic designer – Chris George – for designing the book graphics and tolerating my many requests for variations and adjustments. I love what we've created!

- To my proofreaders and copy editors – Jessica Montanez and Kyle Woodley – for patiently waiting for me to get it done and your thorough review once I did. You have taught me, once again, how to improve my writing.

- To my fellow trainers, speakers, and colleagues – Lucy Brazier, Kemetia Foley, Bonnie Low-Kramen, Cindy Pfennig, Chrissy Scivicque, Laura Stack, Lisa Van Allen – who have provided valuable expertise, insights, and friendship throughout the writing process.

- To all of the administrative professionals worldwide who shared your two biggest challenges when you visited AllThingsAdmin.com. Your willingness to share what is creating frustration and stress in your daily work inspired every chapter of this book. Thank you for being part of the inspiration I need to continue creating training and resources to help you succeed. Because of you, I get to do what I love every day!

END NOTES

1. P-Touch / Brother International Corporation, "Whitepaper: The Costs Associated with Disorganization", 2010. http://www.brother-usa.com/Ptouch/MeansBusiness/whitepaper.pdf.

2. Ibid.

3. Ibid.

4. Joyce v. PepsiCo, Inc, Wisconsin Circuit Court, Jefferson County, No. 2009CV000391. See also: http://www.reuters.com/article/us-pepsico-judgment-idUSTRE59R58N20091028

5. Jennifer Snyder, Whitepaper: The Price of Disorganization in the Workplace, www.neatasapin.net, November 2012, http://www.neatasapin.net/The_Price_of_Disorganization_in_the_Workplace.pdf.

6. Janis Petrini, Business Leaders Lose Hours to Disorganization, www.CorporateMagazine.com, July 7, 2011, https://www.corpmagazine.com/human-resources/business-leaders-lose-hours-to-disorganization/.

7. Ibid.

8. P-Touch / Brother International Corporation, "Whitepaper: The Costs Associated with Disorganization", 2010. http://www.brother-usa.com/Ptouch/MeansBusiness/whitepaper.pdf.

9. OfficeMax - 2011 Workspace Organization Survey, January 2011, http://multivu.prnewswire.com/mnr/officemax/46659/docs/46659-NewsWorthy_Analysis.pdf

10. CareerBuilder, Being Perceived as a Hoarder May Cost Workers a Promotion, Finds New CareerBuilder Survey, www. CareerBuilder.com, July 21, 2011, http://www.careerbuilder. com/share/aboutus/pressreleasesdetail.aspx?id=pr647&sd=7/ 21/2011&ed=12/31/2011.

11. Erin Doland, Scientists find physical clutter negatively affects your ability to focus, process information, www.unclutterer. com, March 29, 2011, https://unclutterer.com/2011/03/29/ scientists-find-physical-clutter-negatively-affects-your-ability- to-focus-process-information/ and http://www.ncbi.nlm.nih. gov/pmc/articles/PMC3072218/.

12. Cena Block and Sunny Schlenger, Time & Space Style Inventory Style Guide, 2014.

13. The University of Stavanger. "Better learning through hand-writing." ScienceDaily. ScienceDaily, 24 January 2011, http:// www.sciencedaily.com/releases/2011/01/110119095458. htm.

14. LinkedIn, November 2015, https://press.linkedin.com/ about-linkedin.

Index

Made in the USA
Columbia, SC
19 December 2018